# VOICE
# LESSONS

# VOICE
# LESSONS

## APPLYING SCIENCE TO THE ART
## OF LEADERSHIP COMMUNICATION

*By*

# RONALD CROSSLAND

ISBN: 1470058227
ISBN 13: 9781470058227

# DEDICATION

*To Boyd Clarke, my late business partner and friend.*
*I wish a friend like Boyd upon everyone.*

*And to Georgianne Smith, a brave and dedicated researcher.*

*Both of you were taken from us way too early and we miss you.*

# TABLE OF CONTENTS

# FOREWORD:
# HOW TO USE THIS BOOK

This work is an extension of the previous two editions of *The Leader's Voice* (New York: Select Books, 2002 and 2008). Those editions contained an explanation of the research Boyd Clarke and I conducted and provided exploration of the research results along with a few helpful ideas on how to upgrade your communication ability. Over the years, as I have coached and trained managers in many different fields, I have found there are three kinds of learners for this material.

One kind of learner accepts or rejects concepts at face value. If a concept is accepted, the learner goes straight to its practical application. The second kind of learner likes the how-to lessons but really wants to understand the research behind the lessons in order to broaden his perspective or satisfy his intellectual curiosity. The third kind of learner has to be convinced by the research first and then selectively applies the concepts to his personal experience.

This book is intended to address all three groups. It covers the research and provides some examples of how the science of communication can upgrade your current communication abilities. There are some practical ideas and even exercises you may find helpful. You can also find practical ideas, video examples, and other ongoing research updates at my website, www.roncrossland.com. The science of linguistics and communication is bolstered daily by the prodigiously active fields of psychology, neuroscience, neurobiology, and a variety of social sciences. Many ideas you currently believe about communication are true, and modern research ratifies those beliefs. Many ideas you currently believe about communication are false, and modern research is altering our view and making it more accurate. The problem, for each of us, is that we often do not know which is which. I have had my own preconceptions and even researched opinions that have been updated and changed by modern research, and I am an active investigator in the field.

That's likely the most important reason you need to read this book. It will help you to sort myth from fact, tradition from modern understanding, and current practices from best practices. I work hard to gather, sift, and present what I find is the most important information for working managers. While this book can help anyone in any field, my first audience is those managers who are courageous enough to choose to lead.

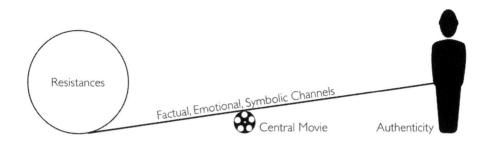

Resistances

Factual, Emotional, Symbolic Channels

Central Movie

Authenticity

# LEADERSHIP COMMUNICATION

British composer John Powell is well known for his movie scores. A member of the Hans Zimmer music studio, he has created music for more than fifty movies, including Shrek, the Jason Bourne films, The Italian Job, Mr. & Mrs. Smith, X-Men: The Last Stand, and the Happy Feet series. He is also the author of How Music Works: The Science and Psychology of Beautiful Sounds from Beethoven to the Beatles and Beyond. In that book he explores and illuminates the art of musical communication via its scientific dimensions, such as the physics of sound and the psychology of hearing musical notes instead of noise. Making these fundamental science attributes come alive, he enhances the experience of listening to, creating, and performing music.

In a similar sense, Daniel Kahneman, Nobel laureate and author of Thinking, Fast and Slow, examines human thinking strengths and weaknesses in psychological and neurological terms. I will reference his work in different places, especially in chapter 6. Other books have been written that show how modern brain science has helped us understand more clearly how our brain works in regard to dealing with emotions, creating strategy, resiliency, physiological processes, immune systems, moral development, and a variety of other topics. Many of these books demonstrate that this scientific understanding can be employed to make your life better if you work at applying the knowledge.

I believe the only way to develop a well-trained leader's voice is to work at it. This book is intended to help you to do just that by telling you about some of the newest and best science about how communication works from a linguistic, psychological, and neurobiological standpoint. Strengthening your artistic communication ability—however developed or undeveloped you believe it to be—by adding a profound scientific understanding will elevate your ability to new levels.

Unfortunately, communication remains one of the most consistently poor competency arenas for managers in the modern world. It is often rated among the top three competencies constituents believe their management does poorly, yet more time and training is spent on strategic thinking skills, project management skills, process management technical skills, financial acumen, or other specific industry competencies than on communication skills. Many revel in their dedication to attaining the next belt in quality training, or in enhancing their customer service scores, while their communication skills atrophy.

There are two types of communicators: those who believe they are above average and those who actually are above average in their communication ability. And as it is with most aspects of leadership, how constituents respond to communication is the relevant measure of one's communication effectiveness. We attempt to cure the communication complaint by either outsourcing our communication to specialists or communicating poorly more frequently. This is like taking an automobile that has difficulty starting to NASCAR engineers for repairs or simply leaving it running all the time because we fear it may not start again.

Communication ability is not window dressing for senior leaders. Every day a leader's voice can "consciously or not, create an intricate web of requests, commitments, assertions, and declarations that affect how people in their organizations act."[1] Getting others to respond to initiatives, decisions, and tasks is what leaders want. And they do so in a highly diverse, and sometimes unintentional, series of speech acts. Our communication through word and deed makes commitments that can inspire or fatigue a constituency. The reality is that constituents really want to respond to the leader's voice, but when the voice is misunderstood, seems erroneous, or simply fails to ignite, they act in ways that are consistent with the misunderstanding, argue for correctness, or feel their motivation begin to degrade. Constituents might act, but often in ways that are very distant from what the leader intended.

Individuals respond to a voice that simplifies the complex and clarifies the cloudy. A voice that quiets dissonance and strikes alignment's chord toward a desirable destination generates a following. We respond to leaders who replace despair with hope, convert cynicism to optimism, and connect activity with meaning.

Few people are gifted with eloquence from birth. Like all leadership competencies, communication abilities must be exercised and developed over a lifetime. In today's world of constant and instant communication, it often seems that eloquence takes a backseat to immediacy, volume, and connection. Rants are often weighed not by their content quality but by their connection volume. Counting blog comments or parading Twitter followers is some people's measure of success, not the content of their communication. But counting how many people are in one's fan base is merely a sophomoric exercise in popularity.

Tirades often seem the only method of gaining attention and increasing one's popular following. Blathering via blogs, emails, newsletters, and town hall meetings is often all the communication hungry get from their leaders. High-definition communication, eloquence dressed in a modern metaphor, cannot be acquired simply by communicating poorly at high volume. Just because leaders seem to spend most of their time communicating or worrying about what to communicate doesn't mean their communication competence increases or their throughput is enhanced.

A well-trained voice can establish a compelling context while others squabble over trivial content. It can challenge others to take a stand during turbulent times. A well-trained voice, amplified by true authenticity, unites a critical mass to move against inertia. A well-trained voice can communicate so compellingly as to raise the consciousness, conviction, and competence of a constituency. High-definition communication may not be your birthright, but if you exercise your artful abilities using the best science, you can increase the quality of your communication.

That's what this book, along with its companion website material, offers: a simple metaphor to remember how to increase your eloquence and direct that eloquence to meaningful leadership tasks. You probably don't need to be convinced of the need to get better at communication, and you may already be using many of the ideas that the best science of communication can offer. For years I did sit-ups every day, but I did them according to the best techniques I had been taught in the 1980s. I now do them every day (well, most days) with techniques illuminated by more recent science, and I get much better results with less effort and fewer unintended problems. This book can do the same for you in strengthening your leader's voice. I am not suggesting you can reduce the time you spend crafting your communication. However, better science is now available that can help make the time you do spend yield better results.

Before launching into the heart of these matters, I want to make two additional parts of the leadership communication story more vivid. Both are patterns that were revealed in a three-year project I undertook that reviewed a century of leadership research.

# Three Eras of Leadership

Communication is the constant companion of three of the four most enduring leadership dimensions studied over the past century. I engaged in a three-year review of the scholarly research on leadership from roughly 1910 to 2010, assessing the meta-patterns of leadership based on research, not on popularized beliefs. I was curious to see which ideas, concepts, and practices of leadership have withstood the test of time. My research uncovered three transitional eras of leadership thinking and four major leadership themes that have proven important in all three eras. The basic findings are outlined in the figure below.

The research review starts in the early twentieth century primarily because before this time leadership wasn't researched using scientific methods. However, many philosophers, leaders, and politicians provided commentary on the subject. Some of it was substantive and insightful; some of it was simply the puffery of egotistical trumpeters of their own success. We get some of both of these in the modern age as well. But since the early twentieth century we have also tried to understand leadership through better methods.

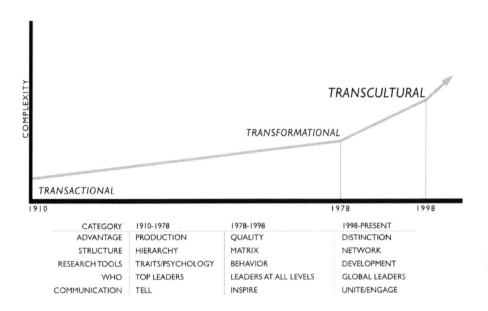

| CATEGORY | 1910-1978 | 1978-1998 | 1998-PRESENT |
|---|---|---|---|
| ADVANTAGE | PRODUCTION | QUALITY | DISTINCTION |
| STRUCTURE | HIERARCHY | MATRIX | NETWORK |
| RESEARCH TOOLS | TRAITS/PSYCHOLOGY | BEHAVIOR | DEVELOPMENT |
| WHO | TOP LEADERS | LEADERS AT ALL LEVELS | GLOBAL LEADERS |
| COMMUNICATION | TELL | INSPIRE | UNITE/ENGAGE |

## Transactional Era

The transactional era lasted for the longest time and covered the dynamic eruptions of two world wars and the Great Depression. Each of these considerable disruptions created the groundwork for later upgrades in thinking about leadership, but during the disruptions and subsequent reconstruction periods, the dominant mode of thinking about leadership was transactional in nature.

Fundamentally, transactional leadership is a mechanistic, utilitarian mode of leadership interaction. The transaction is simple: if you do more for the organization, the organization will offer you more rewards. It's a simple transaction: increased effort yields increased reward.

The conditions facing leaders during this era helped reinforce this leadership mode. During most of the twentieth century, those companies or nations that could produce more gained strategic advantage. Many nations were in the late stages of the second industrial revolution, and their production was assisted by a hierarchical structure that sought to get more done in faster and less expensive ways. To some extent this modality still runs in industry's veins, but there are other complexities that no longer allow it to be the dominant force.

Researchers tended to study famous political or industrial leaders, almost exclusively those at the top. While there were increasing efforts during the 1950s and 1960s to discuss the general "organizational man," most of the study on how to lead centered on senior leaders. And until the late 1960s and 1970s, the primary research tools were biographical sketches, studies of trait behaviors, and applications of various psychological paradigms that competed for explanatory dominance. Even as late as 1985, celebrated researchers were publishing leadership theories for taking charge, a phrase that lends itself to hierarchical structures, that were based exclusively upon interviewing either CEOs or the heads of prominent public sector organizations.[2]

Most communication theory during this time was based primarily on modern reinterpretations of classic rhetoric. In the political sphere the rhetoric was focused on its inspirational tones, but in the commercial sphere there was more emphasis placed on how to tell others what to do, how to do it, and, if need be, why it was important that the work be done. Command-and-control systems tend to view inspiration as a leadership task that surfaces only when circumstances are dire.

# Transformational Era

In 1978 James MacGregor Burns, a Pulitzer Prize recipient and presidential politics and leadership scholar, authored a tome simply titled Leadership. As management by objectives wound down and quality began to eclipse quantity as the primary strategic advantage, Burns elaborated a view that suggested transformational leadership was a more effective paradigm. He expressed it this way: "Such leadership occurs when one or more persons engage with others in such a way that leaders and followers raise one another to higher levels of motivation and morality. Their purposes, which might have started out as separate but related, as in the case of transactional leadership, become fused . . . thus it has a transforming effect on both."[3]

Commercial enterprises experimented with a variety of matrix organizations, structures that aided both the new king of strategic advantage, popularly called the quality movement, and, coincidentally, the advent of transformational leadership. Which came first, transformational leadership or quality circles and matrix management, is a topic that has proponents on both sides.

What is important to the leader's voice, however, is that this era saw a rise in leadership complexity. We began to study leaders at all levels of organization. Project management became a field in its own right. Vision and inspiration came to the forefront of leadership studies as the communication styles of political figures like Kennedy, Reagan, Churchill, Gandhi, and King were studied. Kathleen Hall Jamieson lamented that the growing sound-bite expectation of the general public was squashing the ability of even skilled communicators to present inspirational messages. She contrasted the current standards of televised debates, in which candidates are asked to explain or defend their ideas on a topic in two-to-four-minute time frames, to the Lincoln-Douglas presidential debates, in which each candidate was allotted ninety minutes for a single topic.[4] Frankly it is hard to imagine a commercial enterprise engendering inspiration in a single communication situation bounded by either time range. A few minutes seems like a very short time in which to get an inspirational message across. And to maintain an inspirational message for ninety minutes seems outside modern tolerances and modern leadership capacities. Both time frames can be satisfied. Both require work.

The transformational era was the heyday of leadership competence research. Many researchers attempted to describe leadership in terms of behavioral competence. And many corporations, using less sophisticated scientific methods, set out to demonstrate which competencies were most needed to succeed in their industry. This research netted a consistent domain of leadership competence that crossed industry boundaries. Many suspect that this interpersonal ability, or social intelligence, is the most transportable competency arena for modern leaders.[5] And those who want to cherry-pick the competencies they believe are most useful for their commercial contexts generally have large competency compendiums that allow them to select their preferred subset of leadership competencies.

# Transcultural Era

By the middle of the so-called dotcom era, the general leadership emphasis shifted yet again. Quality lost its dominance as the premier strategic advantage. If you don't have good enough quality in your commercial category these days, you simply will cease to compete. Distinction is now what grants advantage, and that distinction is developed in two ways that are often brilliantly woven together: innovation and brand identity.

Some leaders gain and retain distinction through a reputation for constant innovation, even though each particular generation of product is shipped with known problems. For a time, books on innovation were selling more widely than books on leadership or strategy. Brand identity has been a popular commercial idea for many years, but now brand identity alone can be viewed as the primary reason why some commercial enterprises succeed. It is highly unlikely that the quality of a particular brand of jeans changes depending on whether it is sold through an outlet, discount retailer, or prestige branded retailer. Yet the prestige retailer often claims a larger profit margin than the discounter for the same garment.

Propelled by increasing international competition and the legal requirements for planned leadership succession, developing leaders became the research topic of the 1990s onward. Scholars and consultants by the score offered their own theories and research concerning how to best gain long-term, internal "bench strength." Organizations morphed from matrix organizations to what might be best described as network organizations due to the increasing popularity of virtual workplaces and the technology that enables virtuality. Rank and authority began decreasing as the primary means to stimulate innovation, although, sadly, they are still overused in some contexts. Cross-collaboration and globalization are progressively more stimulating to growth through innovation.

In this transcultural era scholars have also investigated which leadership and communication competencies work cross-culturally. This age hasn't replaced the need to tell constituents what to do and inspire them to want to do it, but it has placed greater emphasis on uniting hosts of "brand-yous," offering them engaging and interesting projects to tackle, and allowing them greater freedom to work on those projects in innovative ways. Developing leaders at every level is an imperative in an age of distance workers, global management, and networked organizations. In my own experience I have encountered many managers who are directly responsible for workers who reside in seven or eight different time zones and who never sit in the same room at any one time. I also have encountered vice presidents who, while they have no one directly reporting to them, are responsible for coordinating the activities of more than a thousand people.

Although research has shown that communication has been important in all three eras, in the current transcultural age the leader's voice stands out as a differentiating skill set. The good news is that the abilities required to lift your voice increase its leverage everywhere in the world. An investment in your voice is an investment in your overall leadership ability.

# The Four Enduring Leadership Domains

In my examination of a century of research, the four most enduring domains of leadership that emerged were:

- Maintaining Credibility
- Moving Forward
- Mobilizing Others
- Molding Structures

Each of these four domains involve two dimensions: the first deals with individual success; the second deals with organizational significance. Leadership successes of great individuals can certainly have impact. We study the personalities of nation-building political leaders such as Sargon I, Qin Shi Huangdi, Pacal the Great, Julius Caesar, Cleopatra, Charlemagne, Pachacuti, Elizabeth I, Catherine the Great, George Washington, and other notable and effective leaders. We also celebrate the commercial leadership of many fascinating individuals as well as the lasting leadership examples of those in the public sector. Although these personal examples are memorable, the organizational leadership capabilities that these individuals brought to bear are often more enduring yet less interesting to leadership development. From athletics to art, music to medicine, education to ecommerce, or performance arts to politics, there are many who aspire and achieve varying levels of excellence. In terms of personal leadership, most leaders have an impact upon some part of an organization; I call this individual success. Fewer make a difference in sustaining the ability of their organizations to endure beyond their leadership tenure. Those who do qualify for what I call organizational significance. At the writing of this book, Steve Jobs has recently passed away. None doubt his personal leadership impact. What remains to be seen is whether or not he left an organization with the ability to endure and remain significant after his tenure.

Many managers work entire careers more focused on individual success as a leader than on overall organizational significance. Most of these managers never rise to the senior levels of an organization that compel them to consider organizational significance as more important than individual success. I don't mean to suggest this arbitrary boundary between senior executives and others means individuals within an organization can't be proud of their organization and work vigilantly to ensure its vitality. But most non-executives are not faced with the same kind of difficult choices over organizational survival as those at the top. And unfortunately the recession of 2008–2010 has revealed numerous leaders who were more interested in personal gain than organizational sustainability or significance.

## Maintaining Credibility

Maintaining credibility is easily divided along the lines of the individual and organization: personal credibility is the responsibility of every aspiring leader, and all employees are charged with upholding the credibility of the organization they serve. Individual leaders, as well as organizations, have brand identities. The question both followers of individual leaders and users of organizational products or services ask is, "Is this brand worth trusting?" In terms of living inside organizations, individual leaders often ask themselves, "Where are the boundaries between me and the organization? Where's the overlap? Do I fit in?" In his book Authentic Leadership, former Medtronic CEO Bill George recounts his development and growth as an individual leader, his company's growth as a brand, and even its battles with the FDA. He declares his beliefs, hard earned over a lifetime of struggle, work, and contemplation, at the beginning of the book: "I believe that leadership begins and ends with authenticity. It's being yourself; being the person you were created to be . . . Authentic leaders use their natural abilities, but they also recognize their shortcomings and work hard to overcome them. They lead with purpose, meaning, and values . . . Authentic leaders are dedicated to developing themselves because they know that becoming a leader takes a lifetime of personal growth."[6]

Peter Georgescu, former CEO of Young & Rubicam, elevates this perspective: "Success now has as much to do with who you are, the unique and moral character your people bring to their work, and the way it governs the way you care for customers—because that trustworthy character is what customers look for now in a company."[7]

There are two difficult, often divisive, questions each person in an organization must wrestle with and resolve. The first is, "Am I being as honest and trustworthy as I can be, personally, in the job I am employed to do?" The second question is, "Am I holding others in this organization responsible for their honesty and trustworthiness as it reflects upon everyone's work, including my own?"

## Moving Forward

This dimension concerns all nuances of vision, mission, and strategy. While credibility helps us believe in the communicator, moving forward is a huge part of the main message. Destination and strategy require articulation in inspiring and meaningful ways. Lifting constituents' gazes from the plentiful petty concerns of a noisy world and inspiring them to want to achieve a desirable goal is a never-ending leadership task. And that task lies with every individual leader during his or her organizational sojourn. The subject of alignment always surfaces in the discussion of destination setting. And the main leverage factor of alignment is a consistent voice throughout the organization.

The organizational leader constantly deals with alignment's counterpart: adaptation. Most organizations collapse before their time as a result of focusing too much on aligning toward near-term goals and not enough on the long-term.

Enduring organizations cast their current noble efforts against a backdrop of constant change. The expectation of every modern worker is that the future will be different from the present. Organizational leadership stimulates inspired groups to work for short-term goals and maintain a readiness for change.

Moving forward isn't just about creating a stimulating vision and laboriously delineating a strategy. It also concerns the ongoing dynamics of affirming purpose and finding suitable paths that allow the community to live out that purpose. Vision and strategy are key elements of a coherent story, what I term a central movie, that allows leaders to stimulate greater alignment as well as update the coherent story as necessary adaptations to new realities occur. All leaders live, think, and act in a stream of history.

## Mobilizing Others

This dimension is a rich domain that essentially secures and retains rich talent and creates opportunities for groups to work together in a common cause. The individual leader as team builder, coach, and coordinator is a familiar figure. The leader's tasks in this arena are well defined, and a lot of effort is expended in helping individual leaders foster an environment of engagement. Some have even reflected that engagement is not a condition that managers adjust through mechanisms of reward and punishment, but is a right of working in and of itself. When considered this way, communication becomes a key asset for leaders who fan the flames of existing engagement rather than bribing the skills and talents of workers to produce.

The organizational leader creates systemic opportunities for these groups to challenge themselves, flourish, and receive recognition and rewards for their efforts through a system that commends contribution. Beyond maintaining these systems, however, organizational leaders develop systems that perpetuate internal leadership candidates. It has been said that there is no training for becoming a CEO. If that were true, then succession planning would be futile. But developing candidates to reach higher levels of leadership is not only possible, it is also mandatory in this competitive world. Due to the characteristics of a transcultural world, communication becomes more important as the leader ascends in responsibility.

## Molding Structures

This fourth enduring dimension of leadership is more process-oriented than people-oriented. It concerns what blend of hierarchical, matrix, and/or network organizations to create; how to use technology to enable the organization structure to work well; and choosing the balance between face-to-face connections to customers as opposed to virtual connections. Although you never see an Amazon warehouse or employee, you encounter both at Toyota each time you visit a dealership. Both organizations can provide you with a personal level of satisfaction, but they employ two different structural methods. While infrastructure and organizational design does communicate in an indirect manner, it is usually experienced as a pervasive and background communication, not as a particular message from any leader.

The essential communication ingredient, however, parallels the dynamic nature of what many refer to as organizational design. Some proponents suggest design is the primary operational issue that requires mastery. Plenty of others argue that execution is the competency most needed in our fast-paced world. My research concludes that dynamic design and faster execution go hand-in-hand and that the communication quotient required is to help others to understand the nature of the changes, embrace those changes, and be able to explain them to others. The result is an improved design that catalyzes greater execution.

While the leadership literature delineates vision/strategy skills from design/execution skills, many organizational workers tend to hear both messages uttered together. However, as will be shown, when fog descends in an organization, the cry for clarity on where to go is louder than the cry for how fast to travel.

# Communication Connection

The four domains of leadership have endured the scrutiny of a century of research. In terms of individual and organizational leaders, however, three of the four are most powerfully connected to communication. These are depicted in the following diagram.

The connection between communication and these three leadership competencies is direct and has been confirmed by many researchers over the past century. The confusion between these competencies and communication exists because we often think of communication as a separate category in itself, not a crucial subset of all other leadership domains. This historical category separation is understandable, because we tend to think of communication as a separate activity from other behaviors such as thinking, analyzing, and doing. When it comes to leadership, however, a substantial portion of the "doing" leadership is the act of communicating.

Consider these statistics. A study of 472 companies demonstrated that their top three leadership difficulties were a lack of trust in leaders, inconsistent or nonexistent messages about the direction of the company, and a simple lack of visibility of managers.[8] The trust issues stemmed largely from the inconsistent messages and poor leader visibility. Managers were seen as either communicating poorly or not communicating sufficiently. And the lack of communication concerning direction also impinged upon organizational trust. Trust, communication, and direction each affected the other through the leader's voice.

A separate study of ninety thousand managers in eighteen countries found essentially the same phenomena.[9] In this case the leadership deficiencies were more pointedly concerned about uninspired communication, a lack of communication, and the trust issues that ensued from these problems. These problems have led Paul Sanchez of the International Association of Business Communication Research Foundation to remark, "The daily struggles faced by internal communicators worldwide have largely been unaddressed."[10]

What this means is that when a workforce lacks trust in a leader, they discount any communication from that leader. When a leader communicates inconsistently or in an uninspiring manner about the future direction of the company, fog descends and trust wanes. When leaders are not sufficiently visible, meaning they are not in communication with their constituents frequently enough, trust erodes, concerns arise, and engagement wanders.

Research literature richly demonstrates the vital connection between voice and the domains of credibility, vision, and engagement. Trust is an underlying factor in all three and is enhanced by a leader's dedication to frequent, inspiring, and collaborative messages. Erosion in any one of these three areas affects the perceived leadership competency in these three domains. A brilliant strategist who is uninspiring loses significant leverage. A commanding organization builder who spreads his efforts too thin and becomes less visible squanders the leverage of his relationship skills. And the leader who believes he can manipulate his way into trusting relationships will find his career and company compromised.

# Leveraging Your Voice

Archimedes is one of the ancients who discovered the power of simple machines. One of his most famous expressions is "Give me a lever long enough and a fulcrum on which to place it, and I shall move the world."[11] Turning Archimedes's insight into a method of examining your voice can provide a simple mechanism for understanding and retaining a bulk of what my research has to offer. Using the basic components of leverage, consider how they could apply to the study of leadership communication.

In order for a leader to move the world via communication, he must overcome the natural resistance that precedes adoption of a message. The lever he must use consists of three channels of communication: factual, emotional, and symbolic. These must be used in concert for the lever to be long enough. The fulcrum is the central movie, a term that will be further explained. And lastly, the leader must have a place to stand, which is his authenticity.

## Resistance

The first chronic communication obstacle a leader must overcome can be demonstrated by the following often repeated study. Take a scale from "very ineffective" to "very effective" communication with an average spot on the continuum. Ask managers which side of the average line they fall on, and you will find that roughly 80 percent report they are above average. Most of them do not place themselves at the extreme end of effectiveness, but most place themselves above average. The results are a form of confirmation bias. It occurs in nearly all populations of individuals who are surveyed about their communication ability. Most of us believe we are better communicators than we actually are. Most of us believe if there is a communication problem, it lies somewhere else, not with our own communication ability.

Ask constituents to rate their managers using the same scale, and confirmation bias is expressed again. Constituents regard roughly 70 percent of their managers to be well below average to average communicators This means constituents blame ineffectiveness on others, another form of confirmation bias. But 30 percent of managers are judged to rise above average. I have studied this 30 percent for years, and much of this book reflects what I've learned about those we all see as expert communicators.

The second chronic communication obstacle you must overcome is congeniality bias. The stronger your beliefs about important ideas such as business, politics, religion, education, marriage, and so forth, the more resistant you are to hearing information that is contrary to your beliefs. People look for information that bolsters their strongly held beliefs at twice the rate they look for and evaluate evidence that goes against them. When it comes to our most fervently held beliefs, we start discounting contrary evidence the moment we encounter it.

The third chronic communication problem leaders must overcome is what my late partner, Boyd Clarke, and I termed the "four fatal assumptions." In some ways these stem from the first two problems. After a leader communicates, usually she automatically and unconsciously assumes the following:

1. Constituents understand the communication
2. Constituents agree with the communication
3. Constituents care about the communication
4. Constituents know how to act upon the communication

These are insidious and dangerous assumptions, and in our fast-paced world we employ them every day.

These three chronic obstacles must be overcome in every situation. For many situations the context of the communication exchange is familiar enough that even when one of the obstacles obscures a communicator's intent to a degree, the constituent can use his own experience and sensibilities along with situation familiarity to override the obstacle. To count on this, however, is dangerous. Many a communication error has occurred when one party hears what he believes to be a familiar utterance, only to later find the communication was interpreted in a totally different way.

# Central Movie (Fulcrum)

People are often bothered by questions of why. Why do I exist? Why do people do the things they do? Why do I work at this job? Why do I have these relationships? Why is my society not living up to its ideals? The neuroscience behind this incessant attempt to answer the "why" questions will be covered in subsequent chapters in more detail, but for now let's accept the general principle that our brains will not stop searching for answers until these issues of purpose have at least an adequate, and hopefully profound, answer.

One of the main purposes of the leader's central movie is to answer why questions. Central movies offer an explanation of the main context, the big ideas, the meaning behind the activity. They answer the question why we have decided to go to a certain destination and why the selected route has advantages over other routes. They answer the question of how we will not only conserve valued principles, but also, perhaps, enhance the principles to new levels of understanding. Central movies are how individual leaders, during their short-lived tenures, put voice to enduring ideological issues that generally outlive any one person.

History is littered with examples of memorable sound bites that attempt to etch in memory some of the answers to why questions. One of the principles former British prime minister Margaret Thatcher constantly had to challenge was gender equality, saying, "You may have to fight a battle more than once to win it."[12] She embodied the struggle for gender equality, which was furthered by her election and tenure.

Nelson Mandela, tough, visionary, savvy, and practical, led his country from a jail cell and then as an elected official in South Africa. "Education is the most powerful weapon which you can use to change the world,"[13] he once said, and in a variety of ways he has both embodied this ideal (having earned his law degree while in jail) and promoted it as a primary method for uplifting people to a higher plane of moral purpose and relationship building.

Ho Chi Minh is not a name often cited in American books on leadership, since he was on the opposing side of a bitter conflict. But having studied his speeches and life, I understand that the most powerful theme of his general central movie, the theme that held his nation together during a long and brutal conflict that started well before U.S. involvement, concerned national pride: "It was patriotism, not communism, that inspired me."[14] Minh's rhetoric often leans on the ideal that what the Vietnamese most wanted was their own freedom from the French, the Chinese, and the Americans.

Ronald Reagan often expressed opinions like, "Man is not free unless government is limited."[15] Reagan's central movie is laced with arguments that the federal government of the United States impeded more than it helped, and he offered a constant reminder of this point of view.

John F. Kennedy is remembered for a variety of reasons, but one of the most important parts of his central movie concerned public service for the betterment of mankind. His words, "Ask not what your country can do for you; ask what you can do for your country," and "If a free society cannot help the many who are poor, it cannot save the few who are rich," are memorable sound bites that express an important tenet of his central movie.[16]

And as a final example, Aung San Suu Kyi, the long-imprisoned social leader who fights against the destructive military government of Myanmar, has said, "Fear is a habit, and I am not afraid."[17] Her learned ability to face great fear with peace and passive resistance earned her a Nobel Prize and has helped her central movie to be heard around the world.

I have purposefully chosen these well-known political and social leaders for three reasons. First, they are individuals with generally well-known histories. Secondly, each of them took a stand for ideals and attempted to influence others who already believed in these ideals to take action. And lastly, each of them have moved constituents to more fully consider their personal beliefs, worldviews, and actions as far as their ideals. This is what a well-trained voice can do. Through the power of developing a strong central movie, which may have four or five major components, leaders create powerful messages that lead others to reconsider their own minds.

I have chosen the "central movie" metaphor for reasons that will become more apparent in chapter 2. For now consider it as a substitute for other ideas such as images, imagery, meaning making, or high-definition communication. Basically the four or five components of your central movie are the fundamental ideas you know you will need to communicate over long periods of time. You will refer to them during emails, one-on-one conversations, while conducting group meetings, and certainly as you address audiences outside your organization.

## Lever (FES Channels)

The primary focus of this book involves the three channels of communication: facts, emotions, and symbols. Research shows that the best leverage leaders have is to use the three channels in concert all the time. When leaders rely too heavily on one or two of the channels rather than using all three in well-developed ways, they shorten their leverage. And as Archimedes and others have demonstrated, even with the best place to stand and a great fulcrum, you will still not move a group to action if your lever is too short.

The good news is that most people use all three channels, whether they think about their communication in those terms or not. The best leaders have learned to use these channels better than others. The intention of this book is to help you to improve your leverage as a leader.

## Authenticity

A credible expert, such as a doctor, may simply offer testimony to the validity or accuracy of a set of circumstances or a body of knowledge. A family member, neighbor, or employee who tells the truth and remains sufficiently honest and open can gain your trust, which lends that person credibility. In neither of these cases do you necessarily place this credibility in a leadership context. Trustworthiness and expertise are the building blocks of credibility, but credibility alone does not confer leadership status.

Leadership authenticity requires us to consider two dimensions in addition to basic credibility. Leaders serve and support groups who are committed to a cause. The causes can range from political liberation to maintaining a small business, but until you serve a cause you are merely hired help. The third dimension of leadership authenticity is that you demonstrate you are in it for the cause, not just for the money.

The fourth dimension of authenticity for a leader is dynamism, the direct link to your voice. Leaders who serve a cause with honest hard work and unquestioned expertise can move a group toward their goals. Those who develop the dynamic qualities of their voice to unite and engage others in the cause they serve ignite performance to higher levels.

I have already cited George and Georgescu on their views concerning credibility. Other authorities have informed my understanding of leadership authenticity as well. Two who have summed up difficult ideas with eloquent phrasing share the same surname. John W. Gardner, former Secretary of Health, Education, and Welfare, founder of both Common Cause and Independent Sector, and the most knowledgeable person on public sector leadership I have ever met, once told me in person, "Communication between leader and follower is at the heart of everything."[18]

As I got to know Gardner better through personal contact and reading his books on self-renewal, excellence, and leadership, I found he brought a thoughtful and persuasive perspective to the subject of leadership authenticity. His insights were no doubt the product of his own personal education as a psychologist and his tenure as a public sector leader. The essence of his insights has been ratified by scientific research. In his book On Leadership he wrote, "A loyal constituency is won when the people, consciously or unconsciously, judge the leader to be capable of solving their problems and meeting their needs, when the leader is seen as symbolizing their norms, and when the image of their leader (whether or not it conforms to reality) is congruent with their inner life of myth and legend."[19]

While Gardner cast his thoughts in a language reminiscent of the age in which he matured, just before and after World War II, he touches on three essential ingredients:

1. leaders must be seen as competent in their role,
2. they must uphold the values of the constituent body, and
3. they themselves must serve as a living example of the central movie they promote and constituents embrace.

Adding to these basic ideas is Howard Gardner, MacArthur Genius Grant recipient, Harvard professor of psychology, and prolific author. As one of the main proponents of the multiple intelligence theory of the mind, Gardner has written extensively about individuals in leadership roles. He concludes, "The formidable challenge confronting the visionary leader is to offer a story, and an embodiment, that builds on the most credible of past syntheses, revisits them in the light of present concerns, leaves open a place for future events, and allows individual contributions by the persons in the group."[20]

Combine the two and the general thesis is complete: leaders must offer a story that goes along with their personal authenticity, which is rooted in their personal credibility and adherence to normative values. This story, which I suggest is better represented as a central movie, is how they will represent the group's noblest intentions and act as a strategist, visionary, and motivator of the group for the purpose of helping everyone move toward a desired destination. They do not simply analyze and act. They put voice to the story, the inspiring vision, the central movie.

We expect a great deal of different competencies from leaders, but the primary ones we demand are that they offer a coherent story of the future and then embody the elements of that story themselves. It is simply insufficient for leaders to be trustworthy and have great expertise. They must also offer and become an embodiment of the vision and values the group represents and put a well-trained voice to the task of elevating the group's consciousness, conviction, and commitment to the movie they already serve.

From this general outline of offering a movie of the future—which is cast in an arc that includes the past and present, being an embodiment of the vision and values, possessing competencies for the task at hand, and serving those who are already committed to a cause—we can derive the essential elements of the popular topic of executive presence.

At its core, executive presence is the visible representation of the leader who is committed to the proposed central movie. A leader may be judged honest, competent, and a believer in the cause. What brings this to life, what causes others to experience presence is the leader's ability to leverage the energy from where she stands to the group. This requires a dynamic, well-trained voice. All the research conducted on executive presence shines a laser on the singular ability of a leader to communicate in a sincere, confident, and inspiring manner whether she is addressing a single person or the entire constituency. At its core, executive presence concerns possessing a well-trained voice. And the well-trained voice must follow the principles of leverage. The leader must have a place to stand, which is personal authenticity and the visible embodiment of constituent values; the proffering of a story, which is the central movie; and the ability to convey that movie via the best communication leverage, which is grounded in the science and art of facts, emotions, and symbols.

I respectfully take a departure from my late mentor, John W. Gardner, and tend to side a bit more with Howard Gardner in one respect: Leadership is not about gaining a loyal constituency, for that makes leadership a power-based enterprise rather than a service-oriented ideal. Leadership is about uniting and engaging those who are committed to a cause to remain vigilant about their values, to stay open to future courses of action, to believe in and act upon the goals of the central movie, and to lead others in a similar manner. The most inspiring leader is the one who best embodies the movie we already believe in and who moves us to higher levels of commitment and performance through the power of voice.

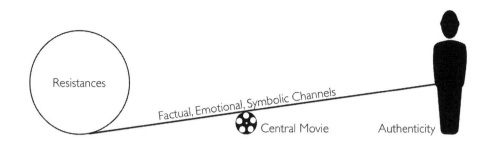

# THE MOVIEMAKING BRAIN

During all moments of consciousness our brains are trying to make sense and meaning of the world. When we experience something and successfully consolidate this experience into memory, we don't just engage in the mindless function of capturing sensory information like a video camera captures sight and sound for exact playback. We add meaning to the experience. When we remember something, we can't replay the memory like replaying a movie or television show, because our brains do not capture information in this fashion. We literally reconstruct or recreate the memory and the meaning of the original experience is a fundamental source of how we recreate the memory. Dean Buonomano, a researcher and professor at UCLA's Brain Institute, concludes, "Information is categorized, grouped, and stored in a way that reflects the world in which we live . . . memory and meaning are intertwined."[1] Making sense and meaning are automatic properties of our everyday mental activities. We connect our sensations, activities, and learning experiences to meaning and memory through the same brain processes. When we remember something, we remember the meaning.

A leader makes a categorical communication mistake if he trivializes this powerful, natural associative functioning of the brain. The brain is obsessed with making sense and meaning. And if leaders want to inspire conviction, align activity, mobilize action, and recognize achievement, they must first help others to create meaning. Joel M. Podolny, Rakesh Khurana, and Marya L. Besharov detail in a lengthy review of the rise and fall of the study of meaning making and economic performance that, "A leader cannot continue to infuse meaning over time unless the organization can survive, and since survival depends on some minimal level of performance, a focus on meaning cannot be maintained to the complete exclusion of a focus on performance."[2] The authors suggest that the study of meaning making and economic performance is a dynamic two-way street. He suggests that linking meaning making to performance is one of the most important activities of a leader.

However, when economic performance becomes the only factor that is meaningful, leaders shrink and weaken their fulcrum, their central movie, to a size and durability that makes it difficult to move the world. Economic performance must surely be *part* of the central movie, but it is simply insufficient to be the *only* theme of the central movie. Our associative brains become dissatisfied and remain so when they see they are only cogs in an economic machine rather than actors in a cause that supplies more meaningful dimensions.

Over the past two decades, scientists have learned more about the human brain than they did in all of the prior two centuries. This pace of research has made it nearly impossible to remain current in the field. Some researchers estimate that 75 percent of what we know about the brain has been learned since 1990. As the brain's complexity has unraveled, scientists have been able to both extend and refine previous theories of the mind. Perhaps more importantly, there has been a revolution in the theories of how the complex structures and pathways of the brain do all the amazing work of providing humans with memory, reason, consciousness, our basic senses, our various intelligences from math to music to athletics, and body regulation. Left brain/right brain models and even the triune brain model have been modified, or replaced, with a more complete picture of how 100 billion neurons do their work. Each neuron connects to as many as ten thousand other neurons, which means the number of different points of contact in the brain is on the order of $10^{12}$ or so—more points of connection than the World Wide Web, and much faster, complex, and adaptable.

It is vital to understand that the human brain is comprised of a variety of powerful systems, each of which plays an irreplaceable role in this process. The brain's associative power, the ability to take inputs from so many different systems and aggregate them, gives rise to one of the most important aspects of brain activity: pattern recognition. Have you ever seen an image appear out of a pattern in a stretch of carpeting or a cloud formation? This everyday phenomenon, called *pariedolia*, is an example of pattern recognition. People see faces on Mars and religious figures on potato chips. Chonosuke Okamura, a Japanese paleontologist, suffered an acute bout of this brain obsession when he claimed he saw many tiny fossils of animals and people, some extinct and some imaginary, in the lines and shading of polished limestone dating from 425 million years ago.

In the same manner, our predilection for pattern recognition and making sense and meaning out of every bit of information in our world leads us to assess why a co-worker made a certain remark or what the boss really meant when he or she didn't make much eye contact during a meeting. People sometimes generate explanations of what is happening that often misinterpret or defy the facts, distort emotional intensity, or misapply symbolic reasoning *rather than go without an explanation.* In my research I have found that leaders who provide information that satisfies this associative, computational, pattern-recognizing brain are considered more powerful communicators than leaders who either don't do so, don't do so very well, or do so in manipulative ways.

For many years, through primary and secondary research, I knew that communicating by using a combination of facts, emotions, and symbols worked better than other methods, but I didn't always completely understand why. The behavioral studies my late business partner, Boyd Clarke, and I completed demonstrated that using these three communication channels in concert provided significant elevations of communication effectiveness; increased a leader's ability to influence others' willingness to act; and established rich, memorable, and effective contextual meaning. When I studied behavior, I understood more thoroughly *what* worked to increase communication ability. When I studied neurology, I gained more understanding in *how* it worked.

It appears there are numerous brain systems that affect factual, emotional, and symbolic communication. These are not the only systems in the brain. Some systems are devoted strictly to the senses—for example, how the eye's lens and retina interact with the visual cortex of the brain to provide our sense of sight. Another example is the automatic systems that regulate breathing and other continuously operating body functions. But many of our neurological systems are involved in supporting the factual, emotional, and symbolic channels of communication that Boyd and I documented. To get a basic understanding of these systems, consider the following three case studies.

# Factual System

The following account is perhaps the best known, most often repeated Ripley's-Believe-It-or-Not kind of story about the brain. Its familiarity still instructs. Phineas P. Gage had a mind-altering experience during the summer of 1848. A dynamic, young construction foreman for the Rutland and Burlington Railroad, he was admired by his colleagues and respected by his crew. Bright, likable, and experienced, he worked tirelessly and thoughtfully at a demanding job.

Clearing the right-of-way along the Black River near the town of Cavendish, Vermont, Phineas prepared areas for detonation by tamping gunpowder into holes in rocky outcrops with a specially designed meter-long iron rod. It was a task that required concentration and precision. One day, as he was pounding gunpowder with his iron rod, he heard a shout and turned his head at the same time he struck downward. With his attention diverted, the rod hit the side of the hole, sparked against the rock, ignited the powder, and the explosion rocketed the iron rod through his left cheek, his left eye, and the top of his head. It whistled through the air and landed dozens of yards away. He was stunned but conscious as his men rushed him to the local town doctor, who stared with amazement at the hole in his head.

Phineas suffered a mild infection, some short-lived fevers, and lost his left eye. Within two months he was released from the doctor's care. That he lived was considered a miracle. After some time off, he tried to return to work. Tests indicated that his memory was intact. He could still count and complete other basic tasks. However, it soon became evident that his personality had permanently changed. He became emotionally mercurial, swaying from indifference to in-your-face-profanity and back. He flitted from one plan to another, never following through. His behavior changed so radically that some former friends had trouble even *recognizing* him in a physical sense. Though he was still physically capable, the railroad let him go because of his dramatic character change. He was no longer the Gage people knew from before the accident. From gaucho, to stagecoach driver, to circus freak, he held many jobs, holding none of them long. At the age of thirty-eight he lapsed into a coma and died.

What happened to Phineas Gage has inspired scientists to consider many specific ideas about his transformation, but all the speculations agree on a major point: the system of his brain that was removed by the rod was a critical part of the logical system, the part of the brain associated with logical reasoning. This loss was substantiated by a wonderful reexamination of Gage's skull, conducted by Hanna Damasio and Albert Galaburda, that revealed with some precision which parts of his brain were removed.[3] Their analysis helped Antonio Damasio conclude that the brain-system loss Gage suffered eliminated a great deal of the cooperation between the brain's logical system and its emotional system. This loss dramatically altered Gage's ability to reason well, to make plans for the future, to stay committed to any course of action for any appreciable length of time, and to function well socially. His brain's ability to make sense and meaning was altered permanently, and the effects of this played out for the remainder of his unfortunate life.

## Emotional System

Antonio Damasio is not only a well-regarded doctor and neurologist but also a gifted writer, who brings complex scientific information to life with terrific stories. One of these, concerning a patient he refers to as Elliot, demonstrates how sense and meaning are altered when a part of the brain's emotional system is lost.

Elliot had developed a tumor in his brain that altered his ability to function in the world. The tumor had not affected his better-than-average intellect; his ability to remember in great detail facts, figures, dates, and events; nor his ability to discuss current politics and business events with apparent ease. His language abilities seemed unaltered, and his physical coordination and functioning worked normally.

The tumor began to change him, however. Just as in the Phineas Gage story, Elliot's basic personality and social abilities were disrupted, and at the time Damasio began to see him, he was already under the supervised care of a sibling. Elliot had lost his first wife to divorce because of his condition, and his very brief second marriage was to a woman many thought an unlikely choice for the pre-tumor Elliot. He drifted about, unable to keep a schedule, wasting his resources, and losing all of his savings to ill-conceived business schemes.

Over a period of testing and reflection, Damasio and his colleague Daniel Tranel found that Elliot had lost his ability to emotionally connect with the world. Tranel presented him with images of earthquakes, fires, floods, and people battered in gory accidents. None evoked an emotional response. Damasio began to form the idea that Elliot could factually know things but not feel them emotionally. Testing his idea, Damasio presented Elliot with a series of problem-solving situations that were comparable to the type of business situations Elliot had been very skilled at before developing the tumor. He easily and readily produced a variety of valid options for each of the situations presented. But after one test session, when finally asked which one of his many options he would pick, Elliot responded, "After all this, I still wouldn't know what to do!"[4]

The loss Elliot suffered shows how important the emotional system is to making sense and meaning in the world. All other functions seemed intact, yet the tumor knocked out his emotional system's ability to coordinate with the others. As a result, Elliot's life was as permanently altered as Gage's.

## Symbolic System

Equally gifted at writing, Oliver Sacks has secured a following for his books on the quirky neurological afflictions that help us understand the brain and the human condition. Inventive book titles like *The Man Who Mistook His Wife for a Hat, An Anthropologist on Mars, and Musicophilia* have attracted and affected thousands who have enjoyed Sacks's poignant observations about the human condition.

One of his stories concerns the tender and fragile events of a patient of his named Rebecca. Clumsy, uncoordinated, possessed of a partially cleft palate, which caused whistling in her speech, and myopic to the point that she required Coke-bottle-thick eyeglasses, Rebecca was unfortunately regarded by others at the time (in the rather politically incorrect terms of the time) as a klutz, moron, and retard. She was shy and withdrawn, as you might imagine, and when Sacks first saw her, when she was nineteen, it seemed she had the intellectual abilities of an eight-year-old.

What struck Sacks and makes his story of her condition so profound was Rebecca's ability to use metaphor, symbols, and stories in a wonderfully poetic manner. Especially when she was presented with calm, soothing surroundings, Rebecca was capable of stitching together the meaning of her life in a warm, lustrous tapestry that allowed her to understand and deal with even the gravest of events. Upon hearing that one of the most important people in her life, her grandmother, had passed away, Rebecca was understandably crushed. She dealt with the sense of this loss through her narrative abilities. When Sacks broke the news to her, he saw her reaction move from a state best described as frozen in grief to one of calm resignation as she cried over the death of her precious grandmother. What she said seems profound for a girl whose overall mental deficiencies were so marked. She first reacted to the news with statements like "Why did she have to go?" and "I'm crying for her, not for me." After this initial reaction, her statements showed acceptance of the situation: "Grannie's all right. She's gone to her Long Home." This poetic idea was followed by "I'm so cold. It's not outside, it's winter inside. Cold as death. She was a part of me. Part of me died with her." After a while a deeper understanding of what had happened and a prediction of the future was revealed when she said, "It is winter. I feel dead. But I know the spring will come again."[5]

Sacks saw in Rebecca the power of the symbolic narrative system, a powerful part of the brain that deals with stories, anecdotes, metaphor, mental pictures, similes, and other symbolic manipulations. Considering Rebecca, Sacks suggested that her case shows: "Very young children love and demand stories, and can understand complex matters presented as stories, when their powers of comprehending general concepts, paradigms, are almost non-existent. It is this narrative or symbolic power which gives a sense of the world—a concrete reality in the imaginative form of symbol and story—when abstract thought can provide nothing at all."[6]

After her grandmother's death, Rebecca rejected any further involvement in the workshops and other treatment processes that attempted to address her non-symbolic abilities. She told Sacks she needed meaning for her life and that the operational classes did nothing for her. As she stood before him, looking down at the carpet in his office, she said, "I'm like a sort of living carpet. I need a pattern, a design, like you have on that carpet. I come apart, I unravel, unless there's a design."[7]

Sacks enrolled her in a theater group that allowed her to thrive. In fact, music and dance seemed to dissolve Rebecca's clumsiness and produce an athletic grace that was not apparent in her everyday activities.

# Brain Update

Three case studies can't confirm a thesis, but thousands of stories ratified by demanding research can and have. These three stories are presented to demonstrate the distinction between the three systems: the factual, emotional, and symbolic. What they illustrate is that although each system can function independently, greater sense and meaning is constructed when all three systems cooperate. Most communication courses are restatements of various portions of these three systems even when they are taught using contemporary, inventive, and delightful language.

Rhetoric is a good subject to study in order to improve your communication abilities. Most rhetorical studies, however, revolve around the basic principles of logos (facts) and pathos (emotions). Symbolism, or what we refer to here as the symbolic system, refers to figures of speech, anecdotes, or stories that simply convey our logic and emotion. Rhetoricians do not generally see symbolism as a separate cognitive agency, but cognitive scientists do. Of course, ethos (the credibility of the communicator) is central to the basic rhetorical coursework. Whether you follow the classic works of Aristotle or the more contemporary versions of rhetoric or communication theory expounded by Kenneth Burke, Geoffrey Hartman, Kathleen Hall Jamieson, Barbara Biesecker, Paul de Man, Jacques Derrida, Marshall McLuhan, or others, you can gain a deeper understanding of what rhetorical theories get right and what they miss by understanding how neurological systems that effect logic, emotion, and symbols work. Sense and meaning are created by the combination of these three systems.

## Your Brain Doesn't Work Like a Computer

To start with, lose the brain-as-computer method of thinking. As Harvard Medical School's John H. Ratey points out, "The brain is nothing like the personal computers it has designed, for it does not process information and construct images by manipulating strings of digits such as ones and zeros. Instead, the brain is largely composed of maps, arrays of neurons that apparently represent entire objects of perception or cognition, or at least entire sensory or cognitive qualities of those objects, such as color, texture, credibility, or speed."[8] Scientists now know that the various lobes (frontal, occipital, temporal, parietal) are more densely interconnected than previously thought and that there is no single center for vision, language, emotion, social behavior, consciousness, or memory. Older models that depict one chunk of the brain taking care of cognition, one taking care of emotion, one taking care of speech and the senses, and one taking care of automatic functions have been left to history's footnotes. Even the search for memory has been dramatically altered, as it is now understood that memories are not stored in a specific area (like a file on a computer) but are literally recreated by combining or recombining information from a vast network of systems. You could say your memory is only as good as your ability to recreate it.

## Incessantly Looking for Sense and Meaning

Secondly, we need to remember that all day, every day, our brains create sense and meaning out of a chaotic world. Neurologist Joseph LeDoux states, "One of the main jobs of consciousness is to keep our life tied together into a coherent story."[9] LeDoux suggests that human consciousnesses requires an explanation of what has happened, what is happening, and what will happen next filtered through an individual's sense of self and her perception of her physical environment. His observations are echoed by the insights garnered by neuroscientist V. S. Ramachandran, who suggests that "the self" has five parts. These parts of the self do the following:

- Create an unbroken sense of past, present, and future.
- Provide a sense of unity—of being one person.
- Connect your mind with your body (which will become important in an illustration later on).
- Establish a sense of agency or free will.
- Provide self-awareness (that is, being able to know that you know).[10]

Making sense and meaning, then, requires being self-aware enough to be able to construct a coherent story about what's happened, what will happen, and what is going to happen to you. These ideas will become very important in our later discussion of how leaders gain alignment to an organization's vision and meaning.

## Brain Movies

A third idea is that since your brain doesn't work like a computer, a different comparison might help us make more sense of how it works. Damasio metaphorically describes brain functioning this way: "Most consciousness studies are actually centered on this issue of the making of the mind, the part of the consciousness puzzle that consists of having the brain make images that are synchronized and edited into what I have called the 'movie-in-the-brain.'"[11] While different from making a Hollywood, Bollywood, or Nollywood (Nigerian movie industry) movie, the movie metaphor does help describe many of the ways in which the brain detects, creates, stores, retrieves, processes, and edits a variety of sensory inputs, memories, mental constructs, logical processes, and feelings. As Ratey puts it, "The brain assembles perceptions by the simultaneous interaction of whole concepts, whole images. Rather than using the predicative logic of a microchip, the brain is an analog processor, meaning, essentially, that it works by analogy and metaphor."[12]

As scientists have unraveled more and more of how the systems work, they have been on a mission to create new mental models that easily explain brain functioning, especially to nonspecialists. Since computer technology leads to erroneous comparisons, the movie metaphor appears to be a new attempt at explaining complexity easily. "Movies are the closest external representation of the prevailing storytelling that goes on in our mind . . . What goes on in the transition of shots achieved by editing, and what goes on in the narrative constructed by a particular juxtaposition of shots is comparable in some respects to what is going on in the mind," Damasio explains.[13]

I have chosen to side with the scientists and use the movie metaphor as a way to help leaders understand that their communication works best when it creates a complete and compelling movie. And it seems that a complete movie uses information from the factual, emotional, and symbolic systems, regardless of what other information is processed. For example, for simplicity's sake, many neurologists present the logical and emotional systems as densely hardwired together. As Richard and Bernice Lazarus point out in their seminal work, "[I]t is a careless—but common—usage to suggest that when we make bad decisions, they are based on emotion, but when we arrive at good decisions, they are based solely on reason."[14] Dr. Daniel Siegel, of the UCLA School of Medicine, is emphatic in his support of this view. "Creating artificial or didactic boundaries between thought and emotion obscures the experiential and neurobiological reality of their inseparable nature."[15] When they are combined, logic and emotion help individuals make the best judgments. As we saw with the Phineas Gage and Elliott stories, if one or the other of these systems is damaged, the ability to reason well drops dramatically.

There are more neurological pathways from the emotional system to the logical system than vice-versa. These pathways interact on every decision. Strong emotion can momentarily overpower our judgments and degrade our decision-making ability. Overcontrolling, denying, or not effectively dealing with emotion can also degrade the quality of our decision making. Or, more important to the emotional or social intelligence theorists, lacking the ability to adequately or maturely process emotion can lead to less effective decision making. As LeDoux's rigorous research shows, "There is but one mechanism of consciousness and it can be occupied by mundane facts or highly charged emotions. Emotions easily bump mundane events out of awareness, but non-emotional events (like thoughts) do not so easily displace emotions from the mental spotlight—wishing that anxiety or depression would go away is usually not enough."[16]

Consider Phineas Gage's story. Critical portions of his frontal and prefrontal logic systems were destroyed by the accident, leaving his emotional system chronically out of touch with his logical system. This eradicated his long-term planning ability. His emotional demeanor and moods turned unpredictable and intense. The emotional system hijacked his life, because it couldn't interact with his logical system. As Ratey explains, "The frontal cortex is the part of the brain that neatly organizes the bits and pieces into a temporal, logical, and 'meaningful' story. However, it must be set in motion by the amygdala, which provides an emotional tag to a memory, a 'meaning' that helps cement the pieces."[17] Gage, once a well-liked, thoughtful engineer with a promising career, lost his ability to create and maintain a movie for his life, because his emotions had no facts or logic to hang on to.

Elliot's story is the reverse. This man lost critical emotional functions through disease, and even though his logical and symbolic systems remained intact, he lost his ability to decide. His logical system could not interact with his emotional system, resulting in chronic indecisiveness, even over trivial matters.

Another series of interesting studies concerns gamblers who have the ability to consistently win at blackjack at such high levels that they are regularly banned from casinos. Studying the logical-emotional connection for these individuals indicates that they seem to have high pattern-recognition and other cognitive skills but low emotional skills. They can win at the game of blackjack but generally are lost in the game of life, unable to form meaningful plans for their lives or sustain important relationships. Many use their winnings so poorly that they are chronically broke. Essentially, if it weren't for blackjack or a similar game of chance, these individuals might just drift through life like Phineas Gage.

It is not just the logical and emotional channels that interact, however. In order for a movie to be made, the symbolic channel must be added. This channel is complex. In the opening chapter we grabbed cupfuls of research from the communication tsunami. Switching metaphors now, here is a collage of quotes about the symbolic channel.

"The ability to perceive objects and events, external to the organism or internal to it, requires images. Examples of the images related to the exterior include visual, auditory, tactile, olfactory, and gustatory images. Pain and nausea are examples of images of the interior. The execution of both automatic and deliberated responses requires images. The anticipation and planning of future responses also requires images."[18]

"Different kinds of memory, like different kinds of emotions and different kinds of sensations, come out of different brain systems."[19]

"Language is, indeed, the ultimate symbolic mental function, and it is virtually impossible to conceive of thought as we know it in its absence."[20]

"You don't have a choice as to whether to think metaphorically. Because metaphorical maps are part of our brains, we will think and speak metaphorically whether we want to or not."[21]

"A key—perhaps the key—to leadership is the effective communication of a story."[22]

"Even the most recondite scientific reasoning is an assembly of down-home mental metaphors."[23]

"Telling stories . . . is probably a brain obsession and probably begins relatively early both in terms of evolution and in terms of the complexity. Telling stories precedes language, since it is, in fact, a condition for language, and it is based not just in the cerebral cortex but elsewhere in the brain and in the right hemisphere as well as the left."[24]

"To this day, nouns are found in the temporal lobe, verbs in the frontal lobe across the Sylvian fissure. It was their coming together that transformed a protolanguage of symbols and signs into a true grammatical language."[25]

"Our whole brain is shaped by language, and many of our cognitive processes are linguistic . . . For us, everything is symbolic."[26]

"We combine symbols to derive layers of meaning."[27]

Rebecca's story above is a poignant example of how metaphor and other symbolism involve a separately functioning mental process that profoundly interacts with the logical and emotional systems, even when the functioning of these systems is compromised.

In summary, a complex series of interactions between the logical, emotional, and symbolic channels combine to create the rapidly changing movie in our minds. We edit the images in a flash, recombine details as new information arrives or is created, and retain information so that when we re-imagine it (re-image it), we can improve our ability to communicate it well. When I found leaders using high-definition communication, it was always composed of information flowing from all three channels. It takes all three channels to form the most compelling image, to complete a movie, to make sense and meaning. Good communicators know how to provide information so that constituents can experience the leader's movie in minute detail in their own minds.

## Filling In the Blanks

Because all three channels are required to make a movie, if a leader doesn't convey information on all three channels, constituents must fill in the blanks from their own mental sources. Steven Pinker points out, "The mind reflexively interprets other people's words and gestures by doing whatever it takes to make them sensible and true. If the words are sketchy or incongruous, the mind charitably fills in missing premises or shifts to a new frame of reference in which they make sense."[28]

This can be a dangerous condition for a communicator. Getting your meaning and message through is hard enough without constituents' minds filling in the blanks. And unfortunately, many of us work under the premise that our memories are infallible, operating like permanently recorded DVDs or computer memory. But that's not the case. Elizabeth Loftus, a noted psychologist and expert on eyewitness testimony, says the following in her article about how people make stuff up if they have to create a memory: "People tend to think of memory . . . [as though] we have all these videotapes of events stored somewhere in the brain if only we can find them."[29] She explains that memories are recreated each time we remember, and that while some memories can be recreated with high fidelity, the reality is that they also change. Ratey explains this in neurological terms: "The formation and recall of each memory are influenced by mood, surroundings, and gestalt at the time the memory is formed or retrieved. Each one arises from a vast network of interconnected pieces. The pieces are units of language, emotions, beliefs, and actions, and here, right away, comes the first surprising conclusion: because our daily experiences constantly alter these connections, a memory is a tiny bit different each time we remember it."[30]

Memory is stimulated constantly through internal and external events. "A memory is only made when it is called upon. We cannot separate the act of retrieving and the memory itself. Indeed, bits and pieces of a single memory are stored in different networks of neurons all around the brain."[31] This process is very complex, as John Medina explains.

Information is literally sliced into discrete pieces as it enters the brain and splattered all over the insides of our mind. Stated formally, signals from different sensory sources are registered in separate brain regions. The information is fragmented and redistributed the instant the information is encountered. If you look at a complex picture, for example, your brain immediately extracts the diagonal lines from the vertical lines and stores them in separate areas. Same with color. If the picture is moving, the fact of its motion will be extracted and stored in a place separate than if the picture were static.[32]

Despite this amazing complexity, our brains retrieve and reconstruct information with good fidelity. When a leader communicates, she is striving to have constituents recall a common memory, to collectively recreate a common movie, whether that movie involves a procedure, policy, strategy, or organizational mission or vision. These conditions lead us to three big ideas about communicating movies:

1. If the leader doesn't provide information on all three channels, constituents will fill in the blanks. It is the only way they can complete their understanding—make a mental movie.

2. Creating high-definition movies in the first place is essential, but it can only occur when the leader uses a good mix of facts, emotions, and symbols when conveying the movie.

3. Repetition of a key message, or central movie (the focus of our next chapter), is crucial to keeping the organization aligned and regulating the natural process that leads individual and organizational movies over time to change—sometimes into movies that are totally different from what the leader is trying to communicate.

## Making Movies

We are all actors in the miniseries of our lives, and work is often a dominant story line. Leaders create an organizational movie of the future and ask constituents to buy in—that's vision. Constituents want a role in a movie that makes sense and meaning to them—that's engagement. Constituents' minds constantly process leaders' descriptions of the future, calls to action, business analyses, or commentaries on hundreds of day-to-day dynamics. As they listen and edit these messages, they recreate (update) or fill in the blanks (originate) a movie that answers questions like:

- How will my job change?
- Can I get this done in addition to all the work I already have to do?

- Does this mean more layoffs?
- How does this new information change what is already going on?
- What opportunities does this provide me?
- How will all of this affect my income?
- Am I capable of what will be required of me?
- What if I fail?
- What if we fail?
- How will we succeed?
- Where are we going?
- Is this worth it?

When the questions are answered and constituents see a role, perhaps a starring role, in this compelling movie, they sign on. Creating alignment, that perennially illusive competence, is simply this: everyone working on and in the same movie. Screenwriting lecturer Robert McKee was interviewed about how to convey powerful business communication.

You [meaning the CEO] say, "Here is our company's biggest challenge, and here is what we need to do to prosper." And you build your case by giving statistics and facts and quotes from authorities. But there are two problems with rhetoric. First, the people you're talking to have their own set of authorities, statistics, and experiences. While you're trying to persuade them, they are arguing with you in their heads. Second, if you do succeed in persuading them, you've done so only on an intellectual basis. That's not good enough, because people are not inspired to act by reason alone.[33]

Alignment is better served by a movie that is meaningful, not just reasonable. Communication flows on three channels: factual, emotional, and symbolic. Any communication that does not adequately attend to one of these channels leaves the leader open to one of the four fatal assumptions of communication. Constituents use their own logic and experience, beliefs and biases to construct sense and meaning. They choose how they view the message and what they will do about it. It is fundamentally important to understand that the only way for the brain to make a movie—that is, to create sense and meaning—is to combine facts, emotions, and symbols. It is how a leader changes the minds of others through producing a shift in their mental representations.

Howard Gardner proposes that seven dynamics are required in order for an individual to change his or her mind. This means a change in the fundamental movie a person believes in, whether it is how to clean the kitchen or whether or not to subscribe to a political or religious ideology. An individual uses the same seven dynamics to change others' minds. Gardner relies upon alliteration as a means of remembering these factors, which are:

- Reason
- Research
- Resonance
- Representational Redescriptions
- Resources and Rewards
- Real World Examples
- Resistances[34]

The subtitle of Gardner's book echoes a familiar theme: *The Art and Science of Changing Our Own and Other Peoples' Minds.* Without going into great detail about mapping his schema onto mine, the parallels are clear. Reason and Research are methods for finding facts and using them well to inform our logical systems. Resonance concerns how to place the information in solid emotional context. Representational Redescriptions (a term Gardner confesses he had to invent to keep his alliteration going) fundamentally refers to symbolic meaning expressed through metaphor and analogy. Real World Examples is about using real stories, illustrations, anecdotes, and case studies. The symbolic channel requires two of the seven in order to be satisfied, which tracks with a great deal of other research. And, of course, Resistances involve overcoming the fundamental resistances reviewed earlier in this book. Gardner does include one element I do not concentrate upon. Resources and Rewards are useful, he says, but unless they align with the other six "Rs," their behavior-altering ability is limited to the expiration of the Resources.

Research conducted on my model of facts, emotions, and symbols reveals the power of their combinatory effect. When a leader becomes better than average at using these channels, he enjoys significant increases in the following:

- Overall communication effectiveness
- The ability to move others to willingly take action
- The ability to influence a change in others' previously held beliefs[35]

This same research project showed that two additional factors were necessary for a leader to command the above results. They had to be perceived as persons of character and credibility, and they had to present an inspiring vision of the future. In a nutshell, this research project demonstrated that when a credible leader relies on a lever of facts, emotions, and symbols and uses this lever against the fulcrum of an inspiring movie of the future, he can overcome the three fundamental resistances of communication, including congeniality bias, which is the most difficult to defeat.

Some people still insist that communication must take on dramatically different forms in different cultures. A group of fifteen researchers working together in China, France, India, Japan, the Netherlands, Singapore, Taiwan, Thailand, Turkey, and the United States embarked on one of the most ambitious studies of influence I've come across. They were interested in resolving two questions. The first was whether or not there was an influence strategy that worked in all the different countries. The second was whether or not there was one influence strategy that worked best in all countries. A rigorous methodology showed that there was one influence strategy that answered both questions, and the influence strategy was to use facts, emotions, and symbols to effect change, secure agreement, or move others to action.[36] While I was impressed by the rigor and difficulty of coordinating such an international study, I was not surprised by the result. These researchers, working from a sociological paradigm, independently verified what cognitive scientists and communication researchers have concluded: to move the world requires making a compelling movie of facts, emotions, and symbols.

# Making Meaningful Movies

If a credible leader uses facts, emotions, and symbols to craft a compelling movie, then the likelihood is greater that the group will participate in a shared movie. Yet within this shared movie, people want to see themselves in the movie. We all want the chance to add a line, a scene, or a plot. As individuals, even when we adopt a shared movie, we reserve the right to confer our personal perspective on it. We want to see that we have touched the movie we see.

We all use these three channels. The trick is learning to use them well, and that requires a well-trained voice. Using these three channels well is like a painter using the three primary colors well, or like a pianist using basic chords well. Three primary colors, and their combinations, create images ranging from doodles to Dalís. Eleven octaves, and their combinations, create piano music ranging from chopsticks to Rachmaninoff's Piano Concerto No. 3, the famous piece that drove Geoffrey Rush's character nearly insane in his Oscar-winning performance in the movie *Shine.* Three channels of communication create meaning ranging from "brush only the teeth you want to keep" to memorable lines like the following from Shakespeare's MacBeth:

> Tomorrow, and tomorrow, and tomorrow,
> Creeps in this petty pace from day to day,
> To the last syllable of recorded time;
> And all our yesterdays have lighted fools
> The way to dusty death. Out, out, brief candle!
> Life's but a walking shadow, a poor player,
> That struts and frets his hour upon the stage,
> And then is heard no more. It is a tale
> Told by an idiot, full of sound and fury,
> Signifying nothing.[37]

Using the three channels well helps constituents imagine a stirring, powerful movie, one that allows them to create personal roles that move the plot along. Most people are looking for a calling, not just a job. We want to defy MacBeth's declaration that life is a meaningless series of events that pass time until oblivion arrives. Alignment occurs not just because the channels were used to invite others to your organization's calling, its mission, or its purpose, but because they were used well, moving constituents to willingly act in a movie worthy of their blood, sweat, and tears.

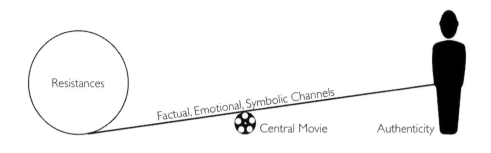

Resistances

Factual, Emotional, Symbolic Channels

Central Movie

Authenticity

# YOUR CENTRAL MOVIE

Dave Browne used to refer to himself as a "numbers only butthead." One of the youngest CEOs I have ever had the pleasure to work with, he was the chosen successor to a charismatic and beloved leader, Ban Hudson, who in the 1990s took LensCrafters from its origins to become one of the most rapid-growing retailers in the United States. Browne is brilliant, has a steel-trap mind when it comes to financial analysis and operational execution, and loves to win.

During the first years of his tenure as CEO, Browne relied only on his MBA-developed muscles. Everyone respected his intellectual prowess and his desire to keep the company moving, but far too many in the company experienced him as an analytic machine rather than a personable leader. His associates respected his authority, valued his business savvy, and described him as an able executive but not an inspiring leader. The passion associates had experienced under Hudson faded to simply going through the motions of best practices as the company's energy shriveled and cynicism found fertile ground.

To his credit, Dave realized he needed to change. His goal of transforming LensCrafters to the next level took the form of first transforming himself. He worked hard at incorporating some difficult upward feedback that Boyd and I facilitated during an offsite into this personal transformation.

Dave got the chance to reveal his transformation during the company's tenth-anniversary celebration. The "Decade II Vision, Mission, and Core Values" event was intended to symbolize both prior accomplishment and shine a light upon the future of "being the best at helping the world to see." The company's newly developed foundation involved providing free eye exams and eyewear to impoverished communities around the globe, and associates lined up to give their time to "giving the gift of sight to those who have the least and need us the most."

Everyone knew that Dave had promoted this effort, but they didn't know how connected it was to his own personal leadership philosophy, because he had never voiced the connection between his innermost beliefs and his actions. In the absence of this connection, people interpreted his actions as simply the means to improve financial performance. He emphasized performance so vigorously that when he did refer to corporate values, many associates felt it was a nod to political corrections rather than a statement of personal connection.

A huge tent stretched over the parking lot of the LensCrafters corporate headquarters, and the occasion was a festival of excitement and pride. Dave took the stage to address the entire group that had assembled to talk about the next decade. But he departed from his usual business style of data recitation and progress updates: he started by talking about himself. He told how he had grown up during hard times in Philadelphia with an immigrant father who worked hard as a mechanic and made the types of sacrifices many immigrant fathers make. His father happened to be in the audience on that day. Dave spoke reverently about his family and his personal faith. He revealed that his desire to win was not going to go away, but he recounted the personal reasons why winning with heart was far more desirable to him than being just another typical Wall Street CEO. He fused the corporate values with his own through a personal message that was liberating for both him and the audience. The standing ovation was a gesture made not only for the continued success of the company but also for the birth of a leader.

From that day forward, Dave developed greater skills at using facts, emotions, and symbols regardless of his message. He revealed his authenticity, posited a few central themes for a central movie, and secured his place to stand. Over time his thematic emphasis solidified and became one with the company, inspiring others to remember and act according to ideals such as "taking the high ground," "giving the gift of sight," "offering legendary customer service," and "being the best at helping the world to see." He cemented his desire to win by the head, by which he meant financial score keeping, with the desire to win by heart, which meant serving his constituency and customers.

## Central Movie Components

Every leader comes to a leadership role with personality, experience, personal values, and a worldview. Leaders vary widely in how much self-awareness they possess, but research has shown that those who spend more time in self-reflection, who regularly explore their personal leadership philosophy, are better able to seek appropriate leadership positions and perform in them. The first component of a well-developed central movie is developing and articulating your leadership philosophy.

The second component of an effective central movie consists of the principles, goals, values, and operating methods of the organization a leader serves. While many values and operating methods are similar across private and public sector organizations, each organization works at developing distinction. Like individuals, organizations want to confer a personal brand identity upon generally accepted ideals.

A leader forges a central movie by blending her personal philosophy with the organization she has chosen to serve. Personal philosophy and organizational philosophy unite through the leader's voice. Sometimes this leads to new expressions of an organization's ideals. Sometimes it ratifies current levels of organizational practices and beliefs. And in some cases a leader must wrench an organization into a new form by advocating a change of values, goals, principles, or operating methods in order to help the organization adapt to new external realities.

# Your Leadership Philosophy

Peter Drucker, the renowned author and leadership observer, once wrote, "The only things that evolve by themselves in organizations are disorder, friction, and malperformance."[1] Drucker wrote clearly and precisely about managerial and leadership tasks for over fifty years. Larry Page, co-founder of Google, seems to prefer less management to the point of promoting self-management fueled by collective inspiration or passion. Many younger leaders of today consider management as something that gets in the way of getting things done.

Perhaps you stand somewhere along this continuum between preferring little or no leadership and valuing highly developed leadership abilities. Regardless of your style, acquired competencies, personality profile, or life experience, you have a view or philosophy of leadership. It may be well formed or something you rarely consider, but it is revealed in every action, in every decision, in every attitude.

Do you know what your philosophy is? Have you made it clear to others? And if you do know, and if you have communicated it, to what degree do you believe it truly represents your deepest considerations on leadership?

John W. Gardner renders a powerful argument for the development of a personal philosophy in his celebrated book *Self-Renewal.*[2] He argues that once a person has passed through the youthful phase of self-identification, personal stakes broaden and deepen. As a leader, at some point you must think and reflect beyond self-interests and self-identification. This means moving beyond how you regard yourself as a leader and considering what your leadership stands for in a larger social context. Gardner promotes and echoes the thoughts of other leadership philosophers who assert that the best leaders seek conceptions of the universe that provide dignity and purpose to everyone.

A person's framework for life is influenced by a number of predictable sources. Family upbringing, educational experiences, social structures, civic and religious influences, athletic endeavors, military service, living in different societies, and work experiences will influence and even inculcate codified philosophies of life, commerce, relationships, and success. Regardless of the ultimate formal philosophy they inherit from work-related or non-work-related sources, each person ultimately reserves the right to confer his or her own personal expression of these acquired frameworks. Each of us has a leadership philosophy, expressed or not, simple or profound.

I suggest you do the deliberate work of grappling with your leadership philosophy. Drag it out of your unconscious and automatic mind. Inspect it. Decipher it. Question it. Debate it with yourself and with others. Examine its roots. Ask yourself if any of it is authentic, or if you are simply mimicking the philosophy you acquired by osmosis. As Peter Koestenbaum exhorts in his workplace leadership philosophy, "Civilization, let alone business, stands or falls on fully understanding and courageously implementing this one point. This insight, before you can fully use it and make it a tool, must be crystal clear to you. [This point is] . . . learning the meaning of personal responsibility and knowing its rootedness in your free will."[3] He argues that personal distinction is the direct result of authentic development applied to a leadership role and implementation.

Koestenbaum's thoughts are consistent with the work of Charles Taylor, Oxford professor and professor emeritus of philosophy at McGill University. Taylor argues that the general unease experienced in modern times has three roots: a loss of meaning due to a fading moral horizon, a loss of vision of the future, and a loss of freedom.[4] Taylor long advocated that individuals examine their personal authenticity against these large-scale aspects of modernity, as these dynamics are part of the globalization we experience in this transcultural age. Leaders regularly influence the sense of a moral horizon by how they speak and act, which promotes meaning in the workplace or stimulates cynicism if their actions are unethical. They are also charged with promoting a sense of shared vision, but as we have already discussed, most of us are pretty lousy at this task. Leaders also directly influence a sense of freedom based upon how they use their influence strategies. Our transcultural age is built upon the prior transformational age, which demoted command and control and elevated inspiring engagement as the preferred leadership competence. At the core of all this activity is the authentic leader.

Rob Goffee and Gareth Jones reiterate this theme. Goffee is a professor at the London School of Economics, and Jones is a fellow of the Centre for Management Development at the London School and a visiting professor at INSEAD. They conclude that the turbulence of modern times has led us all to look for more constancy and meaning in our lives. In terms of business leaders, they suggest, "We've become increasingly suspicious of a world dominated by the mere role player."[5]

They argue with the same observations as Taylor, contending that the ends of modern organizations are defined far too often in financial terms and that the means have become mechanical processes for supporting the ends. The utilitarian mind-set of simple moneymaking leeches meaning and morality from our work life. Goffee and Jones further suggest that although organizations desire leaders, their focus on ends leads to promoting and encouraging conformists or role-players to keep the moneymaking machine going. This basic attitude lends itself even to the leadership-development efforts that organizations embrace. Most leadership development focuses on emulation strategies: finding the characteristics or competencies of financially successful leaders and grafting those skills or personal attributes onto others. Modernity, in the opinion of Goffee and Jones, is not a fertile landscape for growing authenticity. In the end we desire meaning making from our leaders, and we generally only get moneymakers in the role.

Such role-playing leaders are interested only in personal gain bestowed by status, wealth, or power. It can be argued that these dimensions, along with nepotism, seniority, or chance, can grant higher levels of authority and may be prime sources for how individuals scale the corporate ladder. Hierarchical authority and the power that goes with it should not be confused with authentic leadership, however. In fact, financial success should not be so easily regarded as the mono-dimensional indicator of good leadership, as each of the several business cycle downturns since World War II demonstrated.

Manfred F. R. Kets De Vries, who holds degrees in economics and business management and is a practicing executive counselor, writes poetically about the downsides of this type of orientation. He argues that since work is such an important part of how individuals find meaning in the world, leaders need to espouse and embody a sense of values and vision that vigorously promotes a sense of voice and self-determination.[6] As a personal coach and counselor to many CEOs, Kets De Vries has witnessed firsthand how the desire for power corrupts. As for gaining leadership authority through machinations of power, he writes, "Those leaders who are able to combine action with reflection, who have sufficient self-knowledge to recognize the vicissitudes of power, and who will not be tempted away when the psychological sirens which accompany power are beckoning, will in the end be the most powerful."[7]

The most fundamental offering a leader possesses is authenticity. It is what constituents first assess, is most sensitive to aberrations, and most consistently either derails or promotes leaders. Knowing who you are; living with that knowledge; and disclosing it without defenses, camouflage, and pretense is the essence of authenticity. If you put voice to your authenticity in the form of a well-crafted leadership philosophy and then amplify that voice through congruent actions, you have the makings of meaningful and memorable leadership. The essential goal of all leaders is to become more authentic and over time to become the best version of who they really are.

Harry Truman's election campaign experience is one of my favorite historical examples of becoming authentic. Although he was a practiced politician, Truman was not good at presenting a scripted speech. As a president running for reelection, he was often in the position of doing exactly that, however, and his public performances were regarded as stiff and uninspired. Many of his political supporters and critics had been telling Harry what kind of person he needed to be and defined for him what they regarded as the essence of being president.

On April 17, 1948, Truman was speaking at a banquet for the American Society of Newspaper Editors. He had always had a terrific congenial relationship with reporters, who loved the fact that he would speak with them in a manner that was totally different from how he communicated during his speeches. But newspaper editors by and large disliked him and knew him primarily through his public speeches and his political platform. During his campaign eight times as many newspapers favored his opponent, Thomas E. Dewey.

That night he gave a predictable speech that was received with polite applause, a golf clap for the sitting president. But unexpectedly he delivered another, unscripted, impromptu speech. He left his sheaf of speaking notes, moved away from the podium, and addressed the audience authentically. Jonathan Daniels, a journalist and former assistant to FDR, was present at this event. In his book *The Man of Independence,* Daniels wrote,

He began an entirely different, extemporaneous, off-the-record speech of his own, in his own vocabulary, out of his own humor and his own heart. He told the newspapers about his difficult dealings with the Russians . . . He made the story of his problems seem one told in earnestness and almost intimacy with each man in the hall. He was suddenly a very interesting man of great candor who discussed the problems of American leadership with men as neighbors. He spoke the language of them all out of traditions common to them all. When he finished there was a long and loud applause.[8]

Daniels goes on to record that although this speech was well received, it converted only a few. However, Truman experienced his own transformation that night. "The occasion indicated that the native, natural Truman had a gift of speech which was all his own and full of unexpected power."[9]

Truman revealed his voice to himself and to the world that night. He had already forged his leadership philosophy through many years of public service as a senator and then as president by succession upon Roosevelt's death in office. As a first-time presidential campaigner, he listened to others' advice to the point of ignoring his own philosophy, his own voice. In the end he needed only strive to be the best version of himself, despite the odds, and despite expert political advice. From that moment on, Truman connected his voice to what he believed the office of president of the United States demanded. To the surprise of many editors, he won a second term.

# Developing Your Philosophy

A person rises above the trivial when he develops aspirations that are commensurate with what matters to him. The process of maturation or self-mastery has many different theorists and practitioners. In this transcultural era we weigh the benefits of applying best practices leadership competencies to all leaders in an organization rather than helping individuals seek their own process for building their personal strengths. The best aspect of competency models is the verification that statistical analysis of behavior offers. Hopefully you use a competency model with such verification. The worst aspect of competency models is that they smack of Six Sigma machine parts manufacture. Apply the practices to all your managers, and you will upgrade your leadership quotient. Proponents of competency models, like Jim Kouzes and Barry Posner, argue, "When they are doing their best, leaders exhibit certain distinct practices, which vary little from industry to industry, profession to profession, community to community, and country to country. Good leadership is an understandable and universal process. Though each leader is a unique individual, there are shared patterns to the practice of ledership."[10]

Bill George, currently a professor of management practice at Harvard, opposes competency modeling. In an interview at Pepperdine University he said, "I believe a lot of the leadership development work in the eighties and nineties was fundamentally flawed. It took you away from being authentic and tried to socialize you into the normative person."[11] He suggests that the greatest leaders are several standard deviations from the norm and that all of them are authentic, unique individuals whose actions seldom conform to any competency model.

Proponents of the build-your-strengths methodology advocate a well-explored approach to self-development. They advocate building on your strengths and diminishing the effects of your weaknesses. They contend that the time spent in trying to overcome inherent weaknesses is better invested in making progress toward inherent strengths. While in some regards this approach seems sensible, it struggles to allow for an individual's strengths and weaknesses to be modified by time and experience. Most competency models suggest that regardless of your strengths and weaknesses, you should work on improving both in order to become a better leader.

Finding and building upon your strengths has a long heritage, favored by philosophers of earlier civilizations. "At the center of your being you have the answer; you know who you are and you know what you want," Lao Tzu advised.[12] "Be content to seem who you really are," remarked Marcus Aurelius, one of the so-called five good emperors of the Roman Empire.[13] And Thales of Miletus, considered by Aristotle to be the very first philosopher, is believed to have said, "The most difficult thing in life is to know yourself."[14]

These ancient expressions echo through history in modern versions of self-development as the better road to leadership. Marcus Buckingham's self-development tools and working philosophy center on helping others find their core strengths and then matching those to life experiences that will allow their fullest expression. Even in his own life, Buckingham became aware of how different he was from his gifted, mathematically inclined older brother and his naturally athletic sister, and declared, "I was just sure that I was going to get to make my unique mark on the world."[15]

Proponents of this form of self-development suggest that finding your core strengths, focusing on them, and discarding or not worrying about your weaknesses is the best approach. They go so far as to say that in this process you can discover your ability to lead. While Buckingham, Martin Seligman, and Mihaly Csikszentmihalyi are popular authors and thinkers on these matters, all of them owe a debt to Abraham Maslow, one of the modern originators of positive psychology and leadership studies. Most people are familiar with Maslow's hierarchy of needs scale, but that easy-to-remember pyramid was forged from a lifetime of experimentation, research, and insight. The fundamental idea Maslow hoped to spread was this: "The thing to do seems to be to find out what one is *really* like inside, deep down, as a member of the human species and as a particular individual."[16]

There may be opponents to the build-your-strengths, know-thyself, authenticity-striving advocates, but currently their voices are somewhat muted by the enthusiasm for such an approach. Some argue there is no such thing as choosing between competency-based leadership development and strength-based leadership development. One should simply use both. After all, part of finding your strengths is knowing what competencies you already demonstrate at high frequencies. This idea has merit in that exposure to multiple sources of self-discovery is usually a healthy approach to learning more about yourself.

Regardless of your personal bias, consider the forces acting on your development as a person, whether you are in a leadership role or not, as similar to those that act on an airplane. Weight and drag act to keep or move an airplane toward the ground. Thrust and lift act to overcome weight and drag to lift an airplane from the ground to the skies. As we will see in chapter 4, "The Symbolic Channel," "Let's get this off the ground" is a fairly common expression of these dynamics.

Common weights and drags on your leadership ability include fears, phobias, reliance on adolescent coping mechanisms, overconfidence, impatience, inability to trust others, unwillingness or inability to listen to counsel, and other interpersonal bad habits that erode relationships, lower confidence, or promote narcissism. Common components of thrust and lift include courage of convictions, intellectual and social maturity, developing emotional intelligence, forging a personal philosophy, using a well-developed voice to ignite and inspire others, and employing a bias toward diversity in all of its manifestations.

There is sufficient research on these various aspects for a lifetime of study. I recommend that you assess what holds you down or pushes against you as well as what moves you and lifts you and others to action. For the purposes of developing or refining a leadership philosophy that will help you increase the effects of your voice, consider the following recommendations:

1. Data-Mine Your Past Experiences
2. Develop the Habit of Seeking Feedback
3. Explore and Express Your Values

## Data-Mine Your Past Experiences

It is commonly accepted that experience counts in personal development. But not all experiences affect you with the same intensity. Strong emotional experiences, whether momentary or stretched over days and weeks, shape our lives more than ordinary experiences. To help you develop or refine your leadership philosophy, one exercise I recommend is to review your personal history and make a list of the following:

- The three most powerful experiences you've had of being recognized for your work contribution.
- The three most powerful moments you've had when you realized failure was largely a result of something you did or did not do.

- The five people who have had lasting influence over how you view the world.
- The two managers you most want to emulate.
- The two managers you least want to emulate.
- The five books (or authors) that have most influenced your leadership views.

Creating this list will take between twenty minutes and perhaps two hours, depending upon your frame of mind and how easy introspection comes to you. Making the list should be straightforward. Then reflect on how these sources of experience and interaction with others have influenced how you understand your leadership philosophy. This may take several hours or even several days.

The second exercise I recommend is to create four case studies of your own work experience. I recommend recording these case studies as either a written, oral, or video file. Each case study should examine your leadership in the case studies you have chosen. You should recall and record not only what you were supposed to accomplish but also how you went about it, what the general circumstances were, who played influential roles in the experience other than you, and, most importantly, how you think the experience shaped your current leadership perspective or philosophy. Assess to what degree you believe your actions, motivations, interpersonal abilities, or communication skills influenced the situation.

Three of these personal case histories should be about times when you feel you had some measure of success as a leader. It could be the time when you grew sales, improved productivity, opened new markets, shored up a supply chain, increased customer satisfaction, reached a goal despite difficult odds, gained a greater understanding of how to build a team, took a difficult ethical stand, or any of a number of other positive outcomes. One of these three positive experiences should be the earliest experience you had as a leader, regardless of context. Often our early leadership experiences occur while attending school, being part of a civic or religious community, taking on our first job, being part of an athletic team, or serving in the military, all of which can have lasting impact.

Another leadership experience should be either your last leadership role or the a situation you are currently experiencing as a leader. This one might be freshly completed or still under way, but it should be included, as it is shaping your philosophy now. The third experience should fall between your first and most recent, and, again, it can be a leadership experience you have had in any capacity.

The fourth case study should be what you consider a leadership failure. It should reflect a time when you believe that despite your best efforts, or perhaps as a result of your less-than-best efforts, you failed at your leadership role. This might be a clear-cut failure, such as not getting a start-up off the ground, ruining an established business, making a situation go from bad to worse because of your influence, or even simply experiencing a bad year or two during your watch when you simply were not living up to your best leadership abilities. This should be a case study in which you played a role in somehow causing things to get worse, even if there were additional external factors at play.

To sum up this case study exercise, do a deep dive on four personal leadership experiences you have had. The four should be from the following cases:

- Three positive, successful leadership experiences
  - ✓ One of the three being your first success
  - ✓ One of the three being your current or most recent success
  - ✓ One of the three being between your first and last success
- One leadership failure

The third exercise I recommend for examining your leadership philosophy is to carefully and thoughtfully review the material from the first two exercises. Roll the information around in your mind for three or four days or for as long as two weeks. Let it simmer in your mind, but don't overcook it by taking too long. Look for patterns in how you lead, what you feel you have learned, and what aspects of leadership you most are hoping to employ in your current leadership role. Try not to just use the information to confirm what you believed about your leadership ability before you started the exercises, but allow your mind to look for unexpected, even controversial evidence. Then compose an essay that you can email or blog to a group of your peers about leadership. Recording your analyzed and refined perceptions and receiving feedback from those you trust is the reward for all the work you've put into these exercises.

In his book *Strangers to Ourselves*, Timothy D. Wilson presents a powerful argument that there are only two effective means to view your unconscious mind. One is to listen carefully to others' experiences about you and their interpretations of who you are. The second is to be a systematic biographer of your life. Wilson writes, "It is often better to deduce the nature of our hidden minds by looking outward at our behavior and how others react to us and coming up with a good narrative. In essence, we must be like biographers of our own lives, distilling our behavior and feelings into a meaningful and effective narrative."[17] Wilson suggests there is no pipeline to the unconscious, but being a good self-biographer can produce valuable insights.

## Develop the Habit of Seeking Feedback

Introspection and self-biography are half the process. Listening carefully and well to others is the other half of the practice of discovering what you are really like. Marshall Goldsmith is a well-known and very successful senior manager coach. When he engages a new client, he works with that person for a year and gets paid only if the co-workers feel the executive has changed. His advice for how to approach feedback is to consider what he calls The Four Commitments:

1. Let go of the past
2. Tell the truth
3. Be helpful and supportive
4. Pick something to improve yourself[18]

Having a personal coach or mentor enables this process, and for many of us it accelerates the strides we can make in our personal self-development. But you can also do these four things if you develop a sufficiently good relationship with your peers, your boss, and, most importantly, your constituents. It requires more discipline and heartiness to take on some uncomfortable information without a third-party advocate like a coach, but it can be very gratifying. Those leaders who show a greater willingness to be influenced by others when it comes to the weight and drag portions of their character and behavior and who take action to improve based on the feedback gain significantly more influence as leaders than those who don't.

*Letting go of the past* is not easy. Some people believe simple imagery and other self-guided mental techniques can let their prior bad acts drift away like a released helium-filled balloon. If it were that easy, we would not need to include it on a list of habits to develop.

A significant part of letting go of the past concerns the always difficult tasks of asking for others' forgiveness and forgiving yourself. In the workplace saying they're sorry and seeking to repair something they've said or done often feels to leaders like a lessening of their power. Admitting they were actually wrong at some point creates the feeling of a momentary shift in the power balance. And some people have great difficulty in giving up power. They experience it as a confession of weakness or letting go of control, which prompts anxiety in most of us.

Consider asking for forgiveness or apologizing for bad behavior as a way to strengthen a relationship rather than a way of diminishing yourself. Instead of forgiveness being an act of power reduction, it can be viewed as a method for restoring and increasing the power of the relationship, which grants both parties more influence and willingness to work for the good of the relationship. Transformational leadership research has revealed for decades that acts that increase the feelings of power and influence of those on the team or in the group lift everyone to new levels of commitment and power. However, there may be selfish, immature, or cynical individuals who will attempt to take advantage of acts of forgiveness as a means to continue sabotaging your work efforts. If this happens, you may need to exercise other leadership responsibilities.

*Telling the truth* isn't as tricky as some believe. Without getting overly philosophical, most of us in most situations can distinguish between truth and non-truth, between accuracy and embellishment, and between disclosure and withholding. The greatest danger many leaders may experience in the workplace was expressed well by John F. Kennedy: "The great enemy of the truth is very often not the lie, the deliberate, contrived, and dishonest, but the myth, persistent, persuasive, and unrealistic."[19] On many occasions I have consulted with individuals in organizations who falsely believe that they hire the best and the brightest, that their organizational processes are superior to others, and that despite forgivable flaws their senior leaders are the most strategic in the industry. I'm all for positive thinking, but my experiences with these firms suggest that this rhetoric often gets in the way of the truth, especially in terms of leadership development. I am not saying that my client organizations don't have great people—to the contrary, all of my clients have some exceptional leaders. My concern is that false or misguided beliefs in how good we are can build to the level of mythology and obscure truths that could aid in strengthening leaders.

*Being helpful and supportive* is pretty straightforward. Here's how *not* to do it. A colleague of mine recounts a leadership development incident he had with a senior manager. My colleague was in charge of executive development, and his boss agreed to attend a development course that included some hefty and meaningful competency feedback. After the end of the course, the executive stormed into my friend's office, placed the reports on his desk, and growled, "What's the meaning of this?"

My colleague tried to calm his boss down and speak with him about what was truly troubling about the feedback. Although the boss did temper his outburst, he didn't alter his viewpoint. It became clear in the conversation that the boss wanted my colleague to change the views of those who directly reported to him, who obviously didn't understand how to provide feedback that was consistent with the boss's views of himself. It was the end of the boss's development and the introduction of a particularly sour period for the direct reports.

You can be more helpful and supportive than this. Strive to maintain a relationship that is open to feedback, and you will get more honesty. Make individuals feel small, scared, or stunted in career opportunities, and you will get all the positive feedback you ever wanted—it just likely won't be the truth. I once worked with a senior executive who believed injecting doses of fear in his team was requisite for good leadership. He was a brilliant, dynamic man but had not left the transactional era's dependence upon command and control as leadership methods. After receiving some tough competency feedback and both attending and sending all of his direct reports through leadership development training, his behavior changed. At one significant offsite event he distributed Post-it notepads with the heading, "From the desk of God." He told his direct reports that if he deviated from the public declarations he had made as to his intentions to improve as a leader, and if he received written feedback in the form of a sticky note, there would be only thanks and no reprisals. He was as good as his word and altered his behavior.

*Picking something you want to work on* is terrific advice and often overlooked. We become obsessed with what the competency data reveals or with other upward feedback metrics. We overreact to what others think we should work on without relying upon our own healthy intuition and needs. To work only on those things is limiting. To include working on something you are eager to improve is enormously helpful.

## Explore and Express Your Values

The third thing you can do to inspect and develop your philosophy is to explore your core values. There are a number of methods available, from card sorts, to online questionnaires that can help you select from a wide array of human values and select those most meaningful to you, to more interview-oriented methods.

Go beyond simple values selections, however. Ripen your values inspection by considering which of your personal values are being violated when someone attacks your self-esteem, damages your reputation, or otherwise harms you in a psychological manner. Couple this with asking yourself which of your values are being violated when you get upset by proposed legislation, by the repeal of laws you favor, or by seeing someone having his or her rights or values violated. The fundamental idea is to pay attention to which of your personal core values are being triggered when you experience negative events in the world. Consider why this troubles you, and see if you can articulate to yourself and others what values are at stake in regards to the incident.

Once you have identified and refined your personal understanding of your values, broaden your perspective. Consider which of your values might be universal, which might be widespread but not universal, and which might actually be values adopted by a narrow group or perhaps even just yourself. Examining the value you believe in with this scale process allows you to make inferences about how that value will affect your leadership. In those instances where others hold the same value, leadership is easier in the sense that actions that uphold the value are readily seen as worthy, building esteem when a leader performs them.

Ever since one village began trading with another, values clashes have been evident. The transcultural age we live in is the most intense period of both contested and reconciled values the world has yet to experience. There are plenty of values clashes between cultures, but more than ever, at least in the commercial sphere, values are homogenizing. Consider quality and customer service. Businesses often thrive or die depending on the extent to which they back the quality of their goods and services and how they treat customers. One could argue that these qualities were present during the Bronze Age when one merchant exchanged grain for milk. I wouldn't argue, but world commerce today is showing signs of more similar and pervasive themes in the customer service and product quality arenas. Fifty years ago a customer could attempt a product return and face the need to explain exactly what contractual component was breached before she could get a replacement or refund. Today, because of a stronger emphasis on customer service, we can even return opened food items without question. Although this is not true around the globe, the rate of adoption of these kinds of measures indicates they will become commonplace.

While examining and testing your values helps you determine how widely held they are by others, it offers some other, more important returns. First it may ratify the comparative benefits your values offer. It may further allow you to develop greater understanding, tolerance, and perhaps adoption of others' values. And lastly it may help you and everyone else to evolve commonly held values to new levels of appreciation and application. It may even introduce new conceptions of social values or improve social actions against currently esteemed values.

Examining and knowing your values allows you to articulate them to others. I once saw a leader agree to some work with a vendor by sealing the understanding on a simple handshake. The leader and vendor later came into conflict over an aspect of the job that wasn't explicitly covered in the original handshake. The leader asked the vendor to redo some work at no cost, believing it fell under the original contract. I was there when the deal was negotiated, and I felt the leader was overextending his interpretation and basically didn't have grounds to ask for a cost-free redo. The vendor countered with a different view of the deal, and there was a pretty healthy debate that remained civil but reached an impasse.

After a few moments of thought, the vendor acceded to the leader and did the work. The leader was pleased and the two parties engaged in other work over time. I was troubled by this particular exchange, and a few days after the event I was able to ask the vendor about his decision.

"Why did you decide to redo this piece of the project when it was evident the leader was out of line to ask for it?" I asked.

"Well, it was a dilemma," he said. "As a company we have two views that often compete. One is that customer service, even when customers are overbearing, is a good business value to live by. The other is to strike good economic deals without burdening the process with a lot of paperwork," the vendor explained.

"You mean you do all your work without contracts?" I asked.

"Not at all," he said. "Nearly all our jobs start with a proposal and written agreement. But the nature of our business calls for lots of adjustments along the way, and if we redid contracts or went to too much trouble we'd slow the process down, frustrate customers, and not earn money while we waited for decisions. We teach our folks to navigate between the Charybdis and Scylla of customer service and profitability."

"Did you just use a Greek myth as a metaphor?"

The vendor grinned and said, "Yeah. It came up in a meeting one day when the group was talking about this stuff, and our boss used it. It kinda stuck. I know this manager I was dealing with, and while it may have seemed to you he was trying to get something for nothing, in my experience he simply has a different view of what an agreement entails. If I had felt he was truly trying to take advantage, I would not have agreed. Bad business just generates more bad business. But in this case satisfying his expectations was favorable to the long-term relationship without damaging my sense of profit responsibility. And it will definitely improve my communication of expectations with him the next time we do a handshake deal."

This event is like many others I have had that demonstrate the power of leaders having a philosophy and talking about it in expressive ways with constituents. This vendor's leader didn't just laminate values as simplistic inspirational posters hanging on the walls of offices and workplaces. He discussed what the values meant and encouraged workers to use their own levels of understanding to ripen and apply them to work situations. The following chapters will provide more detail of how to use the three channels to express values and everything else a leader must communicate.

# Organizational Philosophy

Earlier I said all leaders think, live, and act in a stream of history. The same is true of organizations. Arie de Geus argues that "Like all organisms, the living company exists primarily for its own survival and improvement: to fulfill its potential and to become as great as it can be."[20] In a type of anthropological analogy, he argues that a company should live up to its potential while considering its political, social, and existential dynamics. One could argue that companies self-actualize in ways that are similar to how individuals do. Living to the fullest extent of possibilities granted during the course of existence is a more robust interpretation of a business than the more typical and narrow economic interpretation that suggests the goal of any company is to maximize its bottom line.

John Micklethwait and Adrian Wooldridge argue even more pointedly not only that companies have lived and acted in a stream of history but also that their very existence has altered history. "The most important organization in the world is the company: the basis of prosperity of the West and the best hope for the future of the rest of the world. Indeed, for most of us, the company's only real rival for our time and energy is the one that is taken for granted—the family."[21] You might even consider that today's companies possess a greater opportunity for immortality than any one human. While this is theoretically accurate, the reality is that the average life span of large-scale companies declined in the period from the transactional to the transformational age and again from the transformational to the transcultural age. Some people suggest that the average life expectancy of an S&P 500 firm is fifteen years,[22] and others suggest that the life expectancy of a Fortune 500 firm is forty-five years.[23] Not many current large companies are more than a century old, even though a noted few have lived for centuries.

Despite current corporate life spans, we do live in an age where more mature companies, at least outside the United States and perhaps the United Kingdom, view their economic goals as long-term value creation, not merely maximizing stockholder value, which is often a more short-term view. Consultants at the global management consulting firm McKinsey and Company argue that "companies dedicated to value creation are more robust and build stronger economies, higher living standards, and more opportunities for individuals."[24] Over the twenty years that these consultants have examined the results of value creation over short-term stock valuation, they have seen significant benefits in value creation. Among the benefits is the ability for the firm to survive longer. It could be that conditions are favorable for many of the large companies to continue going on for decades longer, at least for those that have a longer, more value-oriented view of what it means to be a company.

Others suggest that this transcultural age is a transitional phase fraught with danger. The excesses of the industrial age need to be tamed through creative sustainability measures that by their very nature demand a level of cooperation unparalleled in history between companies and nations. The survival of individuals and companies are now hitched to ensuring that the planet can sustain the presence of both, and it is no stretch to add national politics to this idea. The second phase of this transcultural age will require global leaders whose abilities are not just being economically prosperous in different nations. It will require leaders who can lift the gaze of companies to view profit not as the goal of the company, but as one of the boundary conditions of sustainability. Some suggest that "with nature and not machines as their inspiration,"[25] current leaders need to overhaul their organizational philosophies to more robustly include international collaboration and environmental sustainability measures as primary concerns.

Regardless of your or your company's views on these matters, the reality is that both profit and nonprofit entities now grapple with more than just brand identities. Individuals increasingly react to corporations as personalities. Companies are regarded at the minimum as institutions with social responsibilities and at the maximum as genuine entities with similar rights and responsibilities afforded private persons. Employees and consumers inspect values, strategy, and mission more personally and persistently than ever. As a leader, you must couple this corporate ideology with your personal ideology and give voice to matters further ranging than operational or financial metrics. Those who are best able to communicate vision and values, and to embody these ideas, are regularly counted as abler leaders, even if they have other leadership deficits.

# Crafting Your Central Movie Themes

A central movie is the overarching movie you need all of your constituents to see. It is the movie that will last the longest, that surpasses short-term projects or goals. It is the movie that best reveals the character, mission, values, and personality of the organization you lead. If you can craft three to five memorable themes that you can link to as you discuss or respond to shorter-term matters, you will be able to more effectively remind and encourage your constituents that their work matters. You will be able to show that the small acts of the moment are linked to longer-term expressions of importance.

In the opening chapter of this book I referred to several political figures and aspects of their central movies. Crafting memorable phrases like those I used as illustrations is not easy, but it is within everyone's grasp. You need to expect that it will take awhile to move from the idea you want to convey to the high-definition communication expression that captures your idea in a memorable way.

For example, the celebrated collaboration of John F. Kennedy and his adviser and speechwriter Ted Sorenson yielded some of the most memorable political thoughts in the cold-war era. Kennedy's inaugural address, one of the shortest ever given, and delivered by a man without a topcoat, hat, or gloves in subzero weather while suffering a cold, is replete with pithy, memorable phrases that are not rhetorical window dressing. Kennedy's ambition was to paint his view of American ideals in ways that were as forceful and memorable as he could make them so that he could then get involved with actions that would support those views. The phrase "Ask not what your country can do for you but what you can do for your country" was an idea Kennedy had during his days as a Massachusetts state senator. When he spoke about this one theme of service to the country, it would often take him two or three paragraphs to cover the idea. As he worked with Sorenson to clarify and amplify this idea, he was able to reduce the thought to two or three sentences as he continued in his campaign for office. By the time he was preparing for his inaugural, he and Sorenson had been able to reduce it to a single memorable idea.

On the other side of the American political stage, I found Ronald Reagan did the same during his tenure as governor of California. His Republican ideas became more focused, and by the time he ran for the presidency, his central themes were polished and practiced. Having reviewed several of Reagan's speeches during the research for our thesis, Boyd and I discovered that Reagan used five themes as backdrops to nearly all of his public messages. In our view his enduring central movie consisted of the following themes:

- America's Greatness
- Individual Freedom
- Limited Government
- The Evil Empire
- Hope for Tomorrow

We saw at least three of these themes expressed in his public speeches regardless of the occasion or the other content of his communication. It took Reagan several years to refine these to memorable, easy-to-use themes that made it easier for him to speak impromptu when the occasion called for it and for his speechwriters to work with him or craft speeches for him.

The point is that it takes time and many drafts to get the themes of your central movie whittled down to memorable sound-bite status. And while I believe that is a worthy goal—the exercise of drafting, editing, and redrafting is just like doing sit-ups; you don't get great abs by sitting around—the purpose behind the goal is what is important. And that importance is that you become crystal clear about how you put voice to the organization's values and vision. You must blend what you believe with what the company believes and construct a compelling version of this movie that you can then use to create and sustain the meaning of your work.

Individuals use a variety of techniques to help make the important aspects of their movies memorable. Some use an acronym as a memory aid. Some use pithy quotations from famous or infamous historical figures. Some use memorable graphic or photographic images that stick in the mind, and then they elaborate upon the images to ensure the right message is conveyed. Others use stories, fables, or parables as the primary vehicle for conveying their central movie's theme. Some, as we will see later, use sustained metaphors as a method to make ideas stick.

Regardless of the techniques used, the goal is to become clear that the movie you promote is the movie you embody. You should be able to show that the ideas you communicate are the same ones that guide your actions. And the clearer you become about the ideas, the better you will be able to respond in the moment to questions of procedure, direction, and meaning.

## Central Movies and Time

In chapter 2 I mentioned Joseph LeDoux, V. S. Ramachandran, and Antonio Damasio. These scientists commented on consciousness, one of the most intriguing and debated topics in neuroscience and philosophy. While there is much more to understand, what we know without question is that the human brain constantly seeks and updates answers to four basic questions of meaning:

1. Who am I?
2. What has happened to me in the past?
3. What is happening to me now?
4. What will happen to me in the future?

Meaning over time is a brain obsession. We update our views of what the past has meant to us as we mature, reedit our memories, and consider situations from different viewpoints. Earlier highly charged events can be replaced or modified by more current highly charged events. We all forecast what the future holds, even if we simply express a desire for it to be a journey into the unknown. This time and meaning obsession is described as making movies in the brain. It is a dynamic process of editing, evaluating, reediting, and reevaluating.

For your central movie to have the greatest appeal, the most successful traction, it must be time based. It must answer questions of the past, present, and future in a context of meaning that may cover any or all of a wide array of contexts from economics, security, values retention or promotion, opportunity fulfillment, and others. And it will need to cover a wide array of time periods from why this project needs to be completed by the end of the week to what the company will be like in five, ten, or twenty years. One medical researcher termed this tying together of past, present, and future as a process of creating memories of the future. Think about it. Isn't that what your expectations really are? Ideas of the future that you hope come to pass have been considered memories of the future for nearly three decades.[26]

Mental time travel is automatic and uses the same processing systems regardless of time period. In fact, constructing and evaluating different future simulations appears to influence how we finally understand what is happening to us in the present.[27] Our factual, emotional, and symbolic brain systems weigh in on how we construct meaning in all three time periods, and the process of considering and reconsidering each time period influences a change in the other two. No matter how it appears, there are key differences between past and future memory construction. To create memories of the future, the brain adds to the mix more processing from two brain regions that support the emotional and symbolic systems.

In particular, when communicating about these three time periods, your movie is strengthened if you speak about the past as something that is ongoing, not completed. Or in particular, those parts of the past that you want to see continue should be spoken about in the present tense. Researchers have shown that speaking about past actions as ongoing rather than completed actions promotes future memories of the future that should be acted upon. In their research, William Hart and Dolores Albarracín concluded, "An aspect marker that described experiences as ongoing rather than completed enhanced memory for action-relevant knowledge and increased tendencies to reproduce an action at a later time."[28]

All leaders are charged with answering these time-based questions. While circumstances dictate the rate at which you update your central movies via revised forecast (changing the memory of the future), the idea that we can make announcements about the future once a year or perhaps quarterly is nearly always insufficient to satisfy this brain obsession. Young children invent wild explanations of how the world works. Hourly news updates offer explanations of why the stock market is moving—or not. This obsession never rests. As Michael Gazzagnia concludes, "It is always trying to make sense out of what is going on around us."[29]

From a communication standpoint, the most essential regions that provide the majority of the input to this time-based moviemaking are the factual, emotional, and symbolic systems. This means you need to take your refined themes—those key elements that allow you to create and offer a central movie—and use the powerful three systems as leverage so that you can move the world. Let's consider an example of this.

The breakup of the former Soviet Union, a process that began in the early 1970s and continues in some regards today, has been a major source of change in the central movies of many countries, many newly formed or reformed. Václav Havel, a poet and playwright, was at the center of the central moviemaking for what this change meant for a variety of the countries that undertook to change their memories of the future.

For example, during the Polish solidarity movement period of the 1970s, Havel was part of a group of Czech and Polish intellectuals who agreed to write essays on the meaning of freedom and publish them during the Soviets' resistance to challenges to their regime. Of the twenty committed to the task, only a few of the Czech writers finished, with Havel's work dominating the effort. His essay "The Power of the Powerless" resounded throughout Eastern Europe and offered new hope at a time when people felt hopeless. Zbigniew Bujak, a Solidarity activist, is reported to have said the following about Havel's words:

This essay reached us in the Ursus [tractor] factory in 1979 at a point when we felt we were at the end of the road. We had been speaking on the shop floor, talking to people, participating in public meetings, trying to speak the truth about the factory, the country, and politics. There came a moment when people thought we were crazy. Why were we doing this? Why were we taking such risks? Not seeing any immediate and tangible results, we began to doubt the purposefulness of what we were doing. Shouldn't we be coming up with other methods, other ways?

Then came the essay by Havel. Reading it gave us the theoretical underpinnings for our activity. It maintained our spirits; we did not give up,
and a year later—in August 1980—it became clear that the party appa-
ratus and the factory management were afraid of us. We mattered.[30]

The doubt-turned-to-conviction in Bujak's comments echoes the senti-
ments of others living throughout the Soviet satellite states.[31]

In late 1989 the Velvet Revolution swept quickly through Czechoslovakia.
The handover of power there was easy in comparison to other regions. The
people sought a voice that could explain the changes and pulled Havel onto
the election ticket against his desires and voted him into office as the country's
president. He was a gentle introvert. But he was also a courageous soul who
spoke out against totalitarian power and was sent to jail on several occasions
for dissidence. He was passionate about his causes but preferred to contrib-
ute from the intellectual sidelines. As the *Economist* records in their obituary
of Havel, "His habitual and even plaintive refrain was that he was a playwright,
not a politician. His only desire was for a political system in which he could do
the only job that he felt truly qualified to do. But events brushed such diffidence
aside."[32] The citizenry needed an orator, and Havel was put on the soapbox.
They needed someone to help them make meaning of the change.

A year after being elected to office, Havel gave his first annual update on
what had happened, what was happening, and what needed to happen next.
This speech literally spurred a daylong celebration with thousands of people
singing and dancing in the street. Having had the pleasure of interviewing several business leaders who were there at the time, I believe its impact may have
been more heartfelt and resulted in more immediate action than Martin Luther
King Jr.'s "I Have a Dream" speech.

Havel's words were massively successful in restoring hope for a beleaguered
people who thought, as many in converting countries or companies do, that
the new progressive regime would right wrongs and that economic prosperity would follow as an immediate consequence. While I recommend reading
Havel's speech in its entirety to gather the full scope of his statements and the
eloquence of his thoughts, below is an excerpt from the speech that showcases
the basic metaphorical scaffolding he used to frame his remarks.

Dear fellow citizens,

There used to be a time when this country's president could have delivered the same New Year's Address he had given a year before, and nobody would have noticed. Fortunately, that time has passed.

Time and history have reentered our lives. The bleak skies of dullness and paralyzing inaction have cleared up. And we cannot help but be astonished at the range of possibilities emerging in a truly free political climate, and how it can always produce fresh surprises for us, in the good as well as the bad sense of the word.

Allow me to mention first all the unpleasant surprises the past year has brought us.

Primarily, it has become clear that the legacy of the past decades we have to cope with is even worse than we anticipated or could anticipate in the joyful atmosphere of those first weeks of freedom. New problems are emerging day by day, and we can see how interconnected they are, how long it takes to solve them, and how difficult it is to establish priorities.

We knew that the house we had inherited was not in good shape. The stucco was falling off in places, the roof looked rather dubious, and we had doubts about some other things as well. After a year of examination, we have discovered to our distress that all the piping is rusted, the beams are rotten, the wiring is badly damaged. We know that the reconstruction already planned and anticipated, will take much longer and be much more expensive than we originally believed.[33]

The house metaphor is both common and vividly rendered.

While this much of the passage seems gloomy, Havel continues to march through the very specific accomplishments of the first year: free elections and free speech were established, a constitution was adopted, religious life was restored, support and admiration from the free world was gained, economic reforms were set in motion, and the Soviet army departed. Havel helps citizens see that "much more has been accomplished in a single year than was done over the past forty-two years."[34]

I often assign the entire speech as a lunchtime reading exercise for my workshop participants. Even those with little or no knowledge of Czechoslovakia's political or social issues at the time report the following about the speech and its construction:

1. It is chock-full of facts, emotions, and symbols.
2. It clearly addresses all three time periods.
3. It is inspirational.

This central movie complies with Howard Gardner's view that in order to change people's minds, a leader must "produce a shift in the individuals' 'mental representations'—the particular way in which a person perceives, codes, retains, and accesses information."[35] These mental representations are not just about measuring the activity of movement, often called *execution,* but also about moving toward something so meaningful that it can alter one's mental view.

Back in Czechoslovakia, people felt for the first time in their lives that they had been told the unvarnished truth by a politician—that the future would be bright only if they applied their own hearts, minds, and bodies to the task. And, all things considered, the Czech Republic has been very successful in becoming a stable nation. Memories of the future, fueled by its most powerful companion, hope, stimulated change that was commensurate with expectations.

The moviemaking idea isn't just about creating a stimulating vision and laboriously delineating a strategy. It also involves the ongoing dynamics of affirming purpose and finding suitable paths that allow constituents to live out that purpose. Vision and values are key elements of a coherent story that allows leaders to stimulate greater alignment as well as to update the coherent story as necessary adaptations to new realities occur.

If you are unclear about your personal leadership philosophy and cannot merge that with your organizational philosophy, you limit your ability to create the most powerful central movie possible.

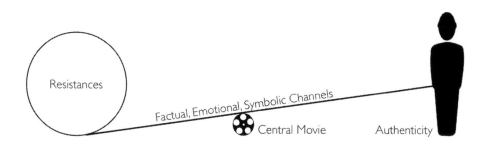

Resistances

Factual, Emotional, Symbolic Channels

Central Movie

Authenticity

# SYMBOLIC CHANNEL

The vast majority of nonmathematical and nonmusical brain systems devoted to the symbolic channel are associated with metaphor and storytelling. Manipulating symbolic language has long been regarded as a high art form, and most people are familiar with a number of rhetorical devices. Here are a few of my favorites:

- Analogy (Knowledge is like a fire; once ignited it burns until the fuel runs out.)
- Alliteration (I'm, like, a little lucky.)
- Antithesis (Success breeds success; failure breeds wisdom.)
- Anaphora (Let freedom ring from Stone Mountain of Georgia, let freedom ring from Lookout Mountain of Tennessee, let freedom ring from every hill and molehill of Mississippi.)
- Consonance (Counting Crows is a cool band.)

- Hyperbole (You use hyperbole a trillion times more than you should!)
- Metonymy (You can't fight city hall. Keep your nose to the grindstone.)
- Oxymoron (He was eloquent in his silence. Our cost-cutting became an expensive habit.)
- Rhetorical Question (Can we progress without change?)
- Understatement (The Great Recession slowed us a bit.)
- Zeugma (In one fell swoop the iPhone put a jukebox in our pocket, a search engine at our fingertips, and reminders in our ears.)

I need to stop before you stop reading. The point of this book is not to turn or return your attention to terms loved mostly by linguists, teachers, and speechwriters. It is to simplify these terms into two major arenas that are far more portable and, in neurobiological terms, more powerful than reliance upon rhetoric for its own sake. Metaphor and storytelling are important methods of increasing communication effectiveness, overcoming congeniality bias, and surmounting the four fatal assumptions in terms of the symbolic channel. Remember, all three channels are required to best overcome the three resistances we might encounter. Generally speaking, the term *metaphor* can branch into specific forms, such as analogy, metonymy, synecdoche, simile, catachresis, and even personification. *Storytelling* takes on the forms of anecdote, case study, narrative, illustration, and parable. From a neurological standpoint, the same systems that give rise to metaphor and storytelling also give rise to the more precise variants of both.

We've already established the brain's obsession with metaphor and story and how the symbolic system helps us move our mental processes to others' brains through the magic of communication. One aspect of both metaphor and storytelling to remember is that these two communication techniques help information stick. They work like Velcro, the fastening product that consists of one pad of tiny hooks compressed onto another pad of tiny loops. You can make Velcro stronger or weaker by the kind of material you use and the density of hooks and loops. In a metaphorical sense (just can't get away from metaphors), you make your metaphors and stories more or less sticky by paying attention to material and the density of hooks and loops. For now, let's consider how to make sticky metaphors.

# Metaphor

Metaphors are not mere literary adornment. They are fundamental to how the brain thinks, evaluates, and then communicates to others a wide variety of mental processes, including mathematical logic. Long taught as a phenomenon separate from logic and analysis, over the centuries humans, especially in Western culture, have created a divide between metaphor and logic that no longer can be supported by research.

Consider this example. Researchers were interested in knowing if a simple metaphor could alter people's reasoning capabilities. They tested several variations of an experiment on how people would think about, discuss, and agree upon appropriate methods for handling crime. Metaphor saturates our daily exposure to this subject as we hear about crime *waves*, killing *sprees*, *epidemics* of criminal behavior, crime *preying upon* a city, *wars* on crime, or indeed communities *infected* with crime. The researchers wanted to know if different metaphorical treatments could influence groups of individuals to reason differently about crime, even when they were given the exact same crime statistics.

In the first round of experimentation the researchers created two groups. One group was asked to imagine a virus infecting a community and then suggest methods for solving the problem. The second group was asked to imagine a wild beast preying on a city and then asked to suggest methods for solving the problem. As you might imagine, the virus group suggested finding the origin of the virus, discovering how it was spread, determining whether or not a vaccine was available or could be created, considering how to develop education about the spread of the virus, and proposing possible hygiene improvements. The wild beast group suggested capturing the animal, caging it, or destroying it. Their suggestions were oriented around organizing hunting parties or hiring animal control specialists to track and stop the beast.

Once the researchers had normalized the ways different groups would handle a virus and a wild beast, they then started their experiments. With new participants, they created two groups. Each group was provided with a report about increasing crime rates in a fictional city and asked for solutions. The difference between the groups centered on the metaphor used to describe the problem. One group's report was laced with virus metaphors. The other report was laced with the metaphor of a wild beast preying on the population.

The virus group proposed investigating the root causes and treating the problem with social reforms such as eradicating poverty and improving education. The wild beast group proposed catching, caging, or killing criminals. Their recommendations were to pass harsher punishment laws. The researchers redid this experiment four times, each time with different groups and each time with one of the following variations:

- Variation 1: Narrowed the metaphors from many virus and beast references to just one short description of each at the very beginning of the report.
- Variation 2: Removed any reference to virus or beast from the report and simply asked the virus group before reading the report to think of a synonym for the virus. They did the same thing with the wild beast group.
- Variation 3: After primed by their separate metaphors, each group was asked to suggest methods for finding out more information about the problem rather than solving the problem.
- Variation 4: Used the metaphor at the end of the report rather than at the beginning to see if doing so produced any changes in outcomes.

What the researchers found is profound. In all cases but the last one, the metaphor induced the virus group to consider increasing education, reducing poverty, and similar proactive measures to reduce crime. And in all cases but the last one, the metaphor induced the wild beast group to consider capture, confinement, and even destruction as appropriate measures. These results occurred even though both groups were provided with exactly the same statistics and information. And even more importantly, *both groups in post-experiment group discussions claimed that their reasoning and judgment was based on the facts, not the metaphor.*

The exception to all of these findings occurred when the metaphor was used at the end of the report. In these cases the metaphorical influence had no effect on either group's reasoning process.[1] The priming did have two additional significant influences, however. The researchers collected data on political affiliation and gender from the participants. They found that generally Republicans and men tended to emphasize law enforcement more than Democrats, Independents, or women. However, when the groups were primed at the beginning, the metaphor influences were significantly stronger in altering people's opinions than either political affiliation or gender biases. This means the metaphor shifted more Republican men in the virus group to consider education and rehabilitation methods than researchers expected. And it shifted more Democratic women toward more law enforcement measures in the wild beast group. This basically means that even straightforward, everyday metaphors can influence a shift in congeniality bias.

Metaphors influence how we begin to think about a subject, how we go about finding out information about a subject, how we come to conclusions about a subject, and how we communicate about a subject. Reactions to the use of metaphorical thinking, reasoning, and communication are not accidental, spurious, or irrelevant. Metaphors are powerful agents that guide our mental and communication processes and should be treated with the same respect shown to numerical analysis, the visual display of quantitative data, and emotional emphasis.

For several decades researchers have considered the power of common, everyday metaphors in the ongoing mental processes that guide and inform our lives. George Lakoff has devoted his life to the study of metaphor influences and has concluded, "Without the metaphor system there could be no philosophizing, no theorizing, and little general understanding of our everyday personal and social lives."[2] He suggests that this neurological system that generates or evaluates metaphor, a significant portion of what I call the symbolic system, is at work during all states of consciousness from totally awake to deep sleep and that we are largely unconscious of the effects. The virus and wild beast study ratifies this idea.

Currently the Intelligence Advanced Research Projects Activity (IARPA) is engaged in a project called the Metaphor Program. This program is based on the idea that metaphors are pervasive in everyday conversation and reveal underlying worldviews and belief systems of the speakers. As Benjamin Bergen, a cognitive scientist at the University of California, San Diego, said concerning IARPA, "They are trying to get at what people think using how they talk."[3]

IARPA is modeled after DARPA (Defense Advanced Research Project Agency), the renowned agency that looks beyond today's needs and requirements to future technologies that will shape the world in general and the Department of Defense in particular. The technology approach IARPA uses data-mines collected and ongoing surveillance information and builds a metaphor database that will more quickly and accurately help the intelligence community maximize their insight and understanding of conversations. Think of it as a type of metaphor-related artificial intelligence. It goes beyond looking for surface details like key words, but dives deeper into understanding through metaphor analysis.

Steve Mithen, of the University of Reading's Department of Archeology, suggests that the ability to reason by using metaphor is part of the evolutionary transition from prehistoric to modern man. He writes, "The transition from Neanderthal man to Cro-Magnon is marked precisely by the ability to 'switch cognitive frames': the Paleolithic blossoming in art may be correlated with the ability to think metaphorically."[4] Lakoff's research demonstrates that our ability to use metaphor and other symbolic language is a powerful and everyday form of our cognitive abilities. "Expressions like *wasting time, attacking positions, going our separate ways*, etc., are reflections of systematic metaphorical concepts that structure our actions and thoughts. They are 'alive' in the most fundamental sense: they are metaphors we live by."[5]

It is a foregone conclusion by researchers in the field that analogical reasoning, meaning our brain's associate processing of information via metaphor and symbolism, is both fundamental and ubiquitous across many mental processes, including problem solving, scientific investigation, causal connections, and, of course, poetry and narrative.[6]

Scientists who often desperately try to avoid metaphor find doing so extraordinarily difficult. Steven Pinker, formerly with MIT and now Johnstone

Family Professor in the Department of Psychology at Harvard University, says, "Even the most recondite scientific reasoning is an assembly of down-home mental metaphors."[7] Susan Oyama, sometimes dubbed as a philosopher of biology, is an outspoken proponent of using great rigor when constructing scientific thoughts and the effect of metaphor upon these constructs. I usually need a dictionary close at hand when reading her work, but she works hard at helping scientists understand how metaphor influences how they frame scientific inquiry. In her book *Evolution's Eye* (an interesting and deliberate metaphorical choice) she writes: "To be sure, scientific metaphors involve not just ways of talking and writing, but ways of seeing and doing. They are implicated in the practices of research, from the initial direction of attention right on to the interpretation, promulgation of results, and application. My choice of title reflects a conviction that one cannot talk about matters of theory and practice without attending to the nuances of language."[8]

Evidence for this use of metaphor abounds. Many researchers suggest that the common, everyday rate of metaphor use is six per minute. That's one metaphor for about every twenty-five words. Referencing Oyama's concern about metaphors in science, the evidence is overwhelming that metaphorical use in the labs helps, rather than harms, successful science investigation. Many scientists are becoming adept at converting from the metaphorical language of the lab to more common metaphors when communicating with mass audiences. Dennis Meredith, a seasoned science communicator who has worked for science labs in prestigious universities such as MIT, Cornell, Caltech, and Duke, and has served on the executive board of the National Association of Science Writers, strongly advises that scientists must increasingly become better skilled at communicating their messages in order to be heard, receive peer reviews, obtain funding, and improve their scientific reasoning abilities.[9]

# Examples of Metaphor

Before proceeding further, let's take a look at some basic, everyday examples of how metaphors lace our speech (note the metaphor). The following quotations were gathered on December 8, 2011, from a variety of sources. As you read each statement, look for the metaphors used.

The European Central Bank embarked Thursday on a series of unconventional measures in a step to fight the euro-zone's debt crisis.[10]

With a swirl of honey-blond hair, feline green eyes and a blue bloodline (her great-grandfather was Marcellus Hartley, the 19th-century philanthropist, whose funeral in 1902 drew Andrew Carnegie and J. Pierpont Morgan), Lauren Remington Platt ticks off all the checkboxes of a successful socialite.[11]

Hong Kong to relax mortgages if economy slumps.[12]

The China Railway High-speed (CRH) train travels at over 300km an hour between Beijing and Taiyuan, capital of Shanxi province. This northern province, with roads congested by overloaded lorries en route for cities, was China's principal coal-producing region for a long time, until it was overtaken by Inner Mongolia. Everything is stained with coal: the sad grey villages, the landscape and the people, whose faces and bodies are blackened from working down [in] the mines. Even the water is black: washing the coal after extraction pollutes rivers and groundwater, making it unsuitable for irrigation or drinking.[13]

Dragonflies have up to 28,000 lenses in each eye—and extraordinary eyesight—but they are "the freaks of the arthropods," [John Patterson] says . . . It is possible that the eyes of Anomalocaris [an extinct creature] had even more than 16,000 lenses—the fossils are detailed, but they are not perfect. In fossil form, the stalked eyes are flattened, like pancakes.[14]

I suspect it was easy for you to spot metaphors in each of these examples. Now let's consider their range and nature. *Embark, fight, relax, slumps, congested, overtaken,* and *stained* are all verbs, or what I call motion metaphors, meaning the metaphorical device is captured in the action described by the verb. *Debt crisis, feline eyes, blue bloodline, freaks of the arthropods,* and *stalked* and *pancake* eyes are object metaphors, or what a language instructor would call nouns or adjectives. The metaphor concerns an object not an action. In some cases the motion and object are linked and can best be understood only when linked, such as *ticks off all the checkboxes.*

It is even easier to spot metaphors when listening to someone talk rather than reading what someone has written. The difference lies in immediacy. Most of the time for some individuals and all the time for the rest of us, metaphors fly out of our mouths unedited when we speak. In conversation we use our previously learned and stored lexicon of expressions to illustrate our mental processes, and they often seem to leap unbidden to our lips. In fact, we are often unaware that we have chosen a particular metaphor when speaking, because we are focused on trying to explain or convey our thoughts about the subject at hand.

Some individuals, often in managerial or leadership roles, rehearse key phrases or even entire speeches in order to refine their ideas and make them more accessible and memorable. We do this more casually when we compose memos, emails, or text messages of various lengths. Writing confers the opportunity for editing before the recipient reads our thoughts. During this editing process we consider and discard a number of different rote metaphorical expressions to arrive at the one that helps us to best convey our meaning. We also edit and discard factual information and exactly how to express any feelings that are pertinent to the subject as well.

Consider another example. This one is a transcript of sixty seconds of speech from the radio show *Science Friday.* Hosted by Ira Flatow, this popular science news program covers a wide range of science and technology topics, often with Ira interviewing notable experts and taking listener calls. This excerpt was about the electricity grid in the United States. Ira was speaking with S. Massoud Amin, professor of electrical and computer engineering at the University of Minnesota and director of the Technological Leadership Institute there. As you read this brief transcript, consider the number and nature of metaphors Dr. Amin used in just one minute of speaking.

Many colleagues or many listeners probably are familiar with the smart meter. They think if I have a smart meter, I have a smart grid. But if you step a little bit out, get a bird's-eye view, you're actually talking about end to end—from fuel source to the end use, from fuel source to your device at home, at work—that is the system. Smart meter is just one node, measurement node, on the customer citizen's interface to the utility. So many of the communication[s] that are the backbone for the communication is fiber optic or microwave, or locally, that is Wifi, Wimax, security built in, security has to be a critical part of this so that it enhances security. It should be built in as a design criteria, not sprinkled on as a condiment or glued on as an afterthought.[15]

Your guess is as good as mine as to which of these metaphorical expressions were immediate, pulled from a rote database of metaphors, and which were more rehearsed and refined. I count eight object metaphors used in this minute of speech, above the six per minute average. Part of my count you may disagree with, as it includes what I call a stylized metaphor. *Smart meter* and *smart grid* are terms that have been invented in the modern age to refer to intelligence in a machine, just like *smart phone*. When first used they were original expressions of a new idea that have become so commonplace that the expression now acts in our speech like an ordinary noun.

In a similar sense the word *threshold* was once a literal description that became a stylized metaphor and eventually became a general metaphorical expression. When most homes had dirt floors, thresh, or straw, was used in the entryway to keep the entry less slippery during the rainy season. A block of wood was used to keep the straw in place, thus a "thresh hold." At the time it was a literal description, but eventually it became a stylized metaphor—nearly all homes had a threshold or entryway to their home, whether they used thresh or not. Then the term became a metaphor for any opening, gateway, or entryway from one place, process, or idea to another.

# Constructing Metaphors

Metaphoric structures are a product of our symbolic system. We use metaphor to think about things, to structure our analysis of events and processes, and they guide the way in which we communicate all of that mental activity. It happens automatically. As a leader, you need to rise above the automatic and corral your metaphoric mental processes. Not only will doing so help you think more clearly or certainly differently, but it also will allow you to convey your ideas more clearly and powerfully to others. Here are three methods that will help you wring more profit out of your metaphors:

- Steal
- Prototype
- Invent

You can remember the three with the acronym SPI. These are formalizations of methods you likely already use casually, but need to use in a more disciplined manner.

## Steal

Stealing metaphors is the most common way adults add metaphorical expressions to their database. (If you don't like the idea of stealing, then perhaps adopt or recycle metaphors will be more palatable). I have often heard participants say if they can leave an educational experience with one good idea, then they have satisfied their requirements for attending. I suggest that among the good ideas you may take away is someone's metaphorical reasoning about a particular subject.

Sometimes the new analogical process will strike a novelty reaction in your brain, which is good for gaining attention. Then as it is used well throughout the meeting or during the speech or as you read about the topic, the novelty will fade as your familiarity with it increases. This is the moment when you need to adopt or steal the metaphor for later use by deliberating embedding it in your own mind. Often this comes in the form of taking mental or written notes of how another person has used the metaphor. Sometimes we retain access by keeping the document we were reading or obtaining notes or slide decks from presenters. The basic idea is that stealing others' metaphors is a great way to improve your own thinking and communication about subjects you find interesting.

Here's an example. For seven years I was the vice chairman of Tom Peters Company. Tom is a genius with language and an unabashed stealer of ideas. In fact he advocates Picasso's style of thinking about the subject of stealing, "Bad artists copy. Great artists steal."[16] (For the rhetoric lovers, this quote is an antithesis example.) But because Tom is always stealing and reinventing himself, he has a history of coming up with new expressions and anticipating new ways of seeing trends in the market.

The August 1997 edition of *Fast Company* had a big bold cover titled "The Brand Called YOU!" Tom coined (or stole and refined) an idea that he explained this way, "Regardless of age, regardless of position, regardless of the business we happen to be in, all of us need to understand the importance of branding. We are CEOs of our own companies: Me Inc. To be in business today, our most important job is to be head marketer for the brand called You."[17]

This was the most often requested reprint from *Fast Company* for several years afterward, and the idea of Brand You became a metaphorical expression of business in the transcultural age. It was so pithy at the time that it collected proponents and detractors by the score. Both parties composed dozens of articles over the ensuing weeks. Arguments broke out. We created a training program around the idea. Some customers loved it. Others wouldn't talk to us about it. Other writers "stole" the idea and expanded upon the implications. Some were already engaged with the same thought processes but had not associated their thoughts with a memorable metaphor. The idea of you being the one in charge of your brand, of that special set of abilities and brand image, has only grown in popularity over time. Brand You is now part of our standard metaphor database.

Steal, adopt, add, increase, or promulgate metaphors you hear or read that you feel better express the ideas, processes, or conclusions your constituents need to consider in order to understand, agree, care, and act. Of course I say "steal," but I don't really mean take a trademarked phrase and claim it is your own. What I mean is to steal in the sense that you use the pithy idea. Literally stealing is wrong and will lead to a world of hurt.

A case that shows how to use the idea well involves an executive I once worked with. His company had bought back all of its shares and had gone private in an effort to gather strength and reposition itself for a future stock market launch. This vice president was a dynamic, action-oriented person who spoke internally to a cross-cultural, educated audience of people who were very used to handling numbers and logical processes but often needed to be stirred to move beyond their analysis to see a larger picture. He often turned to motor racing as an emblem of moving faster in order to win. But he tended to use the metaphor in a one-dimensional fashion, meaning he connected his thoughts only to speed or to winning.

Rather than look for a different metaphorical expression, I worked with him to expand and improve upon the one he had already adopted. Over the course of thirty minutes or so we discussed how other dynamics (motion metaphors) of motor racing might draw parallels to his company's business culture and situation. We found many ideas that could apply, including qualifying races, attaining post position, pit-crew operations and training, gaining sponsorship and endorsements, and using spotters to signal changes in lap strategy that happen very swiftly.

He was delighted with the effort, taking the ideas, putting them in his own language, and drawing his own connections between the extended metaphor and the situation. I later heard that his constituents were significantly impressed with his clarity and enthusiasm. Several commented that based on this one presentation, they had finally put his whole plan together in their minds, something they had struggled to do well in earlier management meetings.

## Prototype

The idea of prototyping applies to nearly everything we do. Humans are continuously working out day-to-day problems by cobbling together wacky ideas or solutions that are designed to solve the immediate task quickly. More refined methods of prototyping involve creating many different solutions to the same problem and gradually narrowing down the candidates to the few that have the most merit. Ultimately one prototype gets advanced over other cases, even if it is difficult to leave behind those that remain.

This process is true of how we communicate on the symbolic channel. When we are explaining, debating, negotiating, arguing, inspiring, or scolding, we use language to try to convey the movies in our minds. We can be effective when we use well-known or commonly held metaphors to convey our ideas. In fact, this is exactly what we do 99 percent of the time. In the moment of preparing to speak, or in the moment of answering a question or responding to a challenge, we answer, and the metaphors already lodged and most used in our database flow through our speech. There is nothing wrong with this.

If you want to up your game, though, you need to prototype—that is, craft and consider—different metaphors that might apply to your situation and select the one that is most powerful for the ideas you are conveying. Here's an exercise that might get you started. Complete the following sentence with as honest and creative answer as you can construct: "Working at my company is like _____."

Pause your reading and give it a go.

Now, before the sticklers reading this get up in arms and remind us that the form of this question is to create a simile, not a metaphor, remember what I proposed earlier. All the creations of the metaphorical menagerie are generated by the same part of the symbolic system. Here are some of the most common responses I get during workshops:

- Bicycle
- Bucking bronco
- Bull
- Rocket ship
- Rollercoaster
- Wave

These ordinary, but useful, metaphors could all be extended for greater effectiveness, as I did with the vice president working on his metaphor of motor racing. More interesting, and therefore memorable, metaphors I've heard are:

- Bucking bronco while trying to email Congress
- Bumper cars wearing blindfolds
- Drunken donkey with a burr under the saddle
- One-eyed burrow
- Schizophrenic elephant
- Steam engine train going up Mount Everest
- Turtle on top of a hoard of snails

As you may imagine, these examples get a few chuckles in a workshop. What's amazing to me is that although some managers enjoy creating such metaphors as a fun mental exercise, many of them are reluctant to use this kind of communication in real life. Granted one needs to be careful in executing a colorful metaphorical phrase because of the dangers of misinterpretation. That's why you need to prototype it, meaning sketch it out fully before you try it out on small audiences to gain reaction. Stretch the metaphor to the breaking point. *All metaphors break down at some point in their comparative ability.* Find the breaking point before you use it, or others will. In fact, by playing around or prototyping the metaphor in advance, you can find out which of the metaphorical connections will not work. This will help you decide the metaphor's usefulness and which of the connections to use and which to avoid.

I once worked with a young financial manager in a new organization who needed to explain her function to a group of engineers who didn't understand nor care much about finance. She needed to convey to them what her varied duties and responsibilities were and why they mattered. We brainstormed a number of different metaphorical structures that might help build a visual image of finance. She started with a shopping center, trying to show how her different functions were like different kinds of retail stores. That was inventive, but it didn't go too far. Next we worked on using bicycles as an illustration. We created a list of different bicycle parts, such as the seat, spokes, brakes, derailleur, frame, reflectors, and handlebars, and then tried to draw parallels to her functions. We made a lot of progress on that one, but I encouraged her to consider one more idea.

"Why, Ron?" she asked. "This one is pretty good, and these guys are engineers, so it should appeal to them."

"True, and it would probably work well," I said. "But try another one simply for the sake of exercising your mind and having a third choice. Our first try didn't go very far, so in a way it was just a warm-up. Don't stop when you get one that works, because a little more effort might help you find one that works even better."

She agreed and we debated two or three other ideas. During this discussion she said she wanted these engineers to most remember that finance was the meat of the enterprise. Without it, you would have a pretty lousy sandwich.

I know from experience that most young engineers like to eat. I stopped our conversation and asked her to go with a hot sandwich as a metaphor. To make a long story short, she used the metaphor of a hot sandwich to discuss the various parts of her work and forged links between expense reporting, forecasting, payroll planning, petty cash, and financial reports to buns, garnish, condiment, meat, and cheese. She called her talk "Building a Profitable Burger." It was a memorable hit.

Here's a method you can use to prototype metaphors. First break down what you want to compare into as many subcomponents as you can. Don't worry if they are the right components. Create an exhaustive list. The second step is to select a potential object from a group of object metaphors. This means you will compare the characteristics of one element to another. Linking aspects of finance to a burger is an example of using an object metaphor. Usually people think through three or four ideas before settling on one metaphor. This mental construction is generally automatic and unconscious, but I urge you to use it more deliberately and consciously. To help you out, here are twenty object metaphors you might want to always have handy for this second step.

1. House
2. Airplane
3. City
4. Chemistry set
5. Automobile or different automobile brands
6. Computers or computer brands
7. Sandwich or pizza
8. Chair parts or types of chairs
9. Human anatomy
10. Brands or types of beverages
11. Bicycle
12. Theme park
13. Animals
14. Kinds or brands of shoes
15. Color wheel
16. Eating utensils

17. Geology
18. Different modes of transportation
19. Writing instruments
20. Timepieces

You could use this list as a stimulus set, simply to arouse your own personal genius. It could be that one of the objects will work well to illustrate the idea you are trying to get across in a more memorable manner. I hope it will do more than this by stimulating you to create new, unique, or more personal object metaphors.

The third step in prototyping an effective metaphor is to list several of the objects' components and start looking for ways of comparing your desired object to one of the object metaphors. Try to make at least five or six linkages or perhaps even more. It is very unlikely you will use them all. You are still in the ideation stage, so more is better. Don't worry about creating an exact fit; for now clumsy is better. You can probably complete this task in a few minutes.

The fourth step is to simply let your mind evaluate whether or not the comparative strength of your metaphor works. Remember, you are trying to make an important idea more memorable by delivering it to others in a way that will make the information stick in their minds. Whether the object metaphor you use is as ordinary as a hamburger or as exotic as the anatomical parts of a mushroom isn't as important as whether or not the comparison is memorable. If you don't like the result, try another. Repeat until you are satisfied.

The fifth step is to rehearse the comparison you have constructed until you feel it is familiar enough for you to use, even if someone attacks the comparative nature of your metaphor. The reality is that all metaphors break down at some point. Using the process above helps you find those breaking points and avoid them, using only the strongest and most memorable connections. In summary, to prototype an effective metaphor, use this process:

1. Create an exhaustive list of the components of the idea, information, or subject you want to explain.
2. Select a potential object metaphor from the twenty provided or ones you like.

3. Make as many comparisons as possible, even if they are clumsy, silly, or ill fitting.
4. Refine the comparison list to a number that serves your purposes and represents your idea well.
5. Repeat the process with another metaphor candidate (or three) just to see if you can do better.

You can use the same process with motion metaphors. These are metaphors that help explain or connect activities, processes, and dynamics. The story of motor racing I mentioned earlier is an example of motion metaphor. Use a familiar process to help illustrate another so that it sticks in your constituents' brains. Here's a list of potential motion- or action-oriented metaphors you may want to have handy.

1. Owning and operating a restaurant
2. Building a house or other structure
3. Launching a rocket
4. Mountaineering (the activities of planning, training, and scaling a mountain)
5. Journeying (the process of discovery)
6. Studying for a test
7. Learning to drive
8. Sailing
9. Flying an airplane
10. Event planning (wedding, graduation, birthday, fund-raiser, etc.)
11. Laboratory experimenting (chemistry, computer, physics, etc.)
12. Writing a book
13. Competing in the Olympics (or other, more local sports activities)
14. Teaching others
15. Preparing for a holiday or vacation
16. House cleaning
17. Race car driving
18. Running for political office
19. Starting a new organization
20. Preparing to live in a new country

Keep in mind that you can combine object and motion metaphors together into a memorable framework. In the year 2000 we celebrated the millennium. Part of the celebration involved list creation. We proposed the top 100 movies of the century, the top 100 music artists, the top 100 most notable figures in history, and so on. One hundred and thirty-seven scholars of history and communication generated a list of the top 100 public speeches made by Americans from 1901 to 2000.[18] Here are the top ten:

1. Martin Luther King, "I Have a Dream"
2. John F. Kennedy, Inaugural Address
3. Franklin D. Roosevelt, First Inaugural
4. Franklin D. Roosevelt, "A Date Which Will Live in Infamy"
5. Barbara Jordan, Keynote to Democratic National Convention, 1976
6. Richard Nixon, "Checkers—My Side of the Story"
7. Malcolm X, "The Ballet or the Bullet"
8. Ronald Reagan, *Challenger* Shuttle Speech
9. John F. Kennedy, Speech to Greater Houston Ministerial Association
10. Lyndon B. Johnson, "We Shall Overcome"

The remainder of the list includes political and social addresses from a variety of public figures, some better known than others. Many, both liberal and conservative, are listed more than once.

I've chosen Reagan's *Challenger* shuttle speech as an illustration of the elegant combining of object and motion metaphors. The overarching metaphor of the speech is pioneering, an appropriate metaphor for both the activities of space exploration and the beliefs most Americans hold about our history as a nation. Without going into a detailed exposition of the speech, since it is readily available for viewing, I will simply list the connections Reagan made between the astronaut pioneers (object metaphor) and pioneering itself (motion metaphor).

| Astronauts | Space Exploration |
| --- | --- |
| Brave, daring people | Hungry to explore |
| Admirable heroes | Prepared for the mission |

| Volunteers | Served the nation |
| Pioneers of Final Frontier | Did jobs brilliantly |
| Emblems of progress | Touched the face of God |

As John Medina writes in his book *Brain Rules*, "[W]e combine symbols to derive layers of meaning. It gives us the capacity for language, and for writing down that language."[19] And turning that written copy into speech.

# Invent

As a science writer, Dennis Meredith understands the need for connecting new phenomena in ways that provide an immediate and portable understanding. When quasars were first being discovered, scientists observed objects jetting narrow streams of unbelievable energy into space. The beams were on the order of six light-years in length and emitted the energy of 10 billion suns. Meredith called them "cosmic blowtorches," and the metaphor stuck. In his description of how neurotransmitters are released from one neuron to another, he coined the term "shotgun synapse" as a way to explain the explosive spray of molecules fired from one neuron to another.[20]

Matt Ridley used the letters of the alphabet, how they construct words, and how words construct chapters in a book to describe DNA in *Genome: The Autobiography of a Species in 23 Chapters*. Nassem Taleb used the story of the black swan and then used this metaphorically in his book *The Black Swan: The Impact of the Highly Improbable*. Peter Georgescu's book *The Source of Success* used the imagery of a source or wellspring that is the beginning of leadership success. Patrick Lencioni is a master of using fable and metaphor in book titles such as *The Five Temptations of a CEO, The Five Dysfunctions of a Team*, and *The Four Obsessions of an Extraordinary Executive*. Warren Bennis used antithesis in *Organizing Genius*, his excursion into describing how the products of genius aren't necessarily random and can be codified. The first business book that enjoyed the same success as popular novels in terms of sales, *In Search of Excellence*, by Tom Peters, used the journey metaphor as an organizing principle. Each of these examples demonstrate inventive means of conveying ideas.[21]

Invention is often the product of sound prototyping. Tom Kelley, one of the minds behind IDEO, a very successful design company, suggested that his company's approach to innovation or invention is part golf swing and part secret recipe.[22] He suggests that the reading, writing, and arithmetic of innovation is prototyping, brainstorming, and observation (please note the metaphorical construction).

I agree with Kelley and recommend this process to you for inventing better and more interesting metaphors. The difference between prototyping and invention is the difference between the known and the unknown. Prototyping revolves around a process of careful comparison of known metaphorical structures. For example, if you were to use beer as the comparison between companies in your industry, you create connections between already known qualities of companies and beer. Invention is taking prototyping to a different level in which you are creating at the minimum a new expression and at the maximum a new category of metaphoric comparison. Prototyping is where you will spend most of your time and is well worth the effort. Invention is more difficult and may or may not work. Like all great invention, though, a good new metaphorical invention is the stickiest metaphor of all.

# 3-D Storytelling

I am going to focus on storytelling as the process of recalling, editing, and conveying prior events or imagining future events as a means to increase event stickiness. I am using the term *event* as a means to convey a focus on things that have really happened, as opposed to the idea of a make-believe story. While stories alone can convey entire messages, most of the time they serve as a means to distill many complex ideas into a consumable, memorable narrative. These features make your story stick, which then allows you to stick more complex ideas to the story, thus making it easier for others to remember.

Your life is a treasure trove of experiences, from the pedestrian to the profound. Whether or not you feel your experiences are worthy as illustrations, case studies, or leadership leverage, the stories of those experiences are a powerful part of the three-channel lever. In my estimation there are three kinds of stories you can relate, all of which can be effectively sticky.

- Personal stories—*This happened to me.*
- Second-person stories—*This happened to someone I know well.*
- All other stories.

Of course you can break any of these three into further broad classifications, such as stories of success, customer service, problem solving, negotiation, motivation, coaching, and so on. The reason I classify them in this manner is because of their relative authenticity.

The closer you are to the action of the story, the more powerful it becomes. While a great many stories about other people from other places, and even other time periods, can be very effectively conveyed, nothing grants more power on the end of the lever than your own personal story. Your authenticity will resonate more forcefully than the great story you tell about your business colleague who saved the day. As human beings we are constantly evaluating the authenticity of those we allow to lead. Telling your personal story helps satisfy this constant leadership assessment. I am not advocating hubris. Personal stories should be used as a way to move others to greatness, not as a means to extol your own greatness. As screenwriter and highly successful screenwriting teacher Robert McKee once told a business audience about storytelling, "Self-knowledge is the root of all great storytelling."[23]

Storytelling is often seen as an entire subject worthy of separate consideration. Many consultants and educators have devoted their lives to helping leaders acquire greater ability in this arena. I praise their efforts. They offer a wide array of views on story classification, story development, and storytelling. If this is an area you want to learn more about, I encourage you to find skilled thinkers and practitioners in this field in addition to considering the research that follows.

Communication leverage is greatest when symbolic channel components like metaphor and storytelling are combined with good facts and genuine emotions. I once worked in an organization in which the senior manager was a gifted storyteller. He could hold audience attention for more than an hour with the down-home stories of his childhood. They were very sticky. But he stuck nothing to them. We in the audience would literally whisper to one another during his presentations, trying to understand where his story was leading in terms of our business, and we found it led nowhere. We called him "the suit with nobody in it." He told terrific stories but with negative leverage.

Some stories are complex and lengthy enough that they contain the relevant information and emotional context to convey an entire message. In a sense the expanded story in this case is using all three channels to make a complete movie. Most of the time, though, we use stories as a method to enhance one aspect of our central movie either as explanation or illustration. This means the story helps us understand the factual logic of a larger issue. This is especially true when you are relating a personal story that stirs others to consider their own personal history.[24] When people are absorbing information that is presented with both factual information and information in the form of a story, if the story prompts them to consider their personal situations, they rely upon the story a bit more to help them decide.

This preference for stories over data is why some people want only the facts and not the story, generally believing that stories distort information and manipulate cognitive abilities. When leaders engage in this behavior innocently we may feel misled but may nevertheless understand the leader's good intentions. At worst, however, we feel conned, and this condition makes all future communications fall under suspicion. As Barry Lopez, a terrific storyteller and a stickler for ensuring that his stories connect to accurate facts, writes, "For a storyteller to insist on relationships that do not exist is to lie. Lying is the opposite of story."[25]

For the moment, I presume you are a leader who refuses to lie, and when you find you have passed along erroneous information, you correct the situation. I will further presume that as a leader you have chosen to embody the very ideas, processes, and values you encourage others to use to make their work lives more meaningful and financial results more robust. With that understanding let's consider the Velcro metaphor as applied to storytelling.

Sticky stories are ones that create Velcro hooks and loops from the story to other information you want to transport along with the story. Any variety of facts or emotions can be stuck to a well-crafted story. Our brains are associative machines, and when we invite one idea into consciousness it arrives with links to other ideas. The Velcro metaphor helps us see how to forge better links from the story to other important information.

Boyd and I played around with a variety of different techniques to make storytelling an easy, practical, and powerful tool for leaders. After some work and research we took all the terrific processes we saw others use, folded in all the research we could find about how the mind uses stories, and boiled it until we reduced it down to three powerful components. These components are:

- Details
- Dialogue
- Drama

We suggest "3-D storytelling" as a process that will make your stories sticky and three-dimensionally memorable.

## Details

The three most important aspects of details are atmosphere, relevance, and order. *Atmosphere* means providing enough extraneous details to give your story a backdrop or body. *Relevance* ensures that the right details in your story hook to the other ideas you want to stick to your story. And *order* simply means relating an event or story in a variety of sequences.

Have you ever known someone who could not relate even a simple experience he had over coffee with co-workers on a given day without rambling on about every unrelated idea, action, or person casually connected with this event? (If you are like this, you may need to work on editing details when using a story for leverage.)

Conversely, you probably know someone who answers in monosyllables about important events. I had a business partner like this once. One day he arrived in the office with a bandaged hand. I asked, "What happened to your hand?" He answered, "Cut it this weekend on some glass." It wasn't until a week later that we all found out he cut his hand on a mirror shard from an auto accident he witnessed. The cut occurred as he helped a small child exit the vehicle as others were assisting the child's bleeding parent from the car. (If you are like this, you may need to work on how to expand your storytelling.)

Some details are not important and do not create hooks and loops. Too many spurious details create only loops on both sides of the Velcro, which reduces stickiness and obscures the hooks you are trying to make. All stories have elasticity, however, meaning the same story can be retold in a thirty-second, three-minute, or thirty-minute version, depending on the occasion. The general difference between these versions has to do with the purpose of the story. Longer business stories are case studies. Shorter stories, like a strip of Velcro, are meant to stick to a more limited amount of information.

Even in the shorter story some details are not hooks but instead provide atmosphere. I occasionally relate the experience of my oldest stepson getting the keys to his first car. I can tell the entire story and make the points that I want without mentioning the following details: my family had always wanted to go to Los Angeles, and in particular my two stepsons had always wanted to go to one of the famous beaches like Laguna, Malibu, or Venice Beach. I can add the details that on my stepson's sixteenth birthday my family traveled to LA, took a limo ride to Malibu, had dinner at a popular restaurant, and as the sun set over the Pacific Ocean my wife presented him with his car keys. None of those details might be particularly important to the hooks of the story I want to make, which is how he had earned the right to a car through his school and community work, how he had been diligent about driver's training, how he had impressed me with his skills as I rode with him during his training period, and how I wanted to make the reward for this effort special. However, the details of a setting sun on a desirable LA beach do help create a certain atmosphere for the story.

The science of stories indicates that it is helpful to forge parallel hooks. The art of stories is to ensure your atmosphere building doesn't become dense fog, obscuring your hooks, but backdrop that provides body. Practice and feedback will inform you if your atmospheric details are working.

The only way you can know if you have *relevant* hooks is to rehearse the story in advance and choose the strongest details that link the story to the nonstory ideas you want people to remember. Here's an example. I once heard an

HR manager discuss how she spent the first eight or nine years of her life in Japan. She loved her life there. As a young girl she made a group of friends, enjoyed school, learned the language, and generally had a happy experience. Her mother organized a party to celebrate the HR manager's sixth birthday and invited her daughter's five closest girlfriends. On the day of the party the friends arrived and brought a baking dish of six cupcakes. Five were white cupcakes with white icing, and the sixth was chocolate with chocolate icing. The HR manager said she asked her friends why the one cupcake was different and they said, "Because you are different. You are black."

This African American HR manager said it was a totally shocking revelation. Until that moment no one had ever treated her differently, and she had not known that others regarded her as being different. As you may imagine, this story has more details and its lingering effects were many. When I heard the story, the HR manager linked the experience to her work on diversity. The points she linked it to were:

1. Sometimes we are different and don't know it.
2. A person's difference can come as a revelation.
3. Your friends are capable of accepting your differences.

As you might imagine, this same story, with various details, could be used to make other points entirely. She could have used this event as a springboard to relate a series of experiences of how she adapted to her new minority ethnic status and how that status changed again when her family relocated to the United States.

Stories often have enough hooks that we have to choose in advance which of them to highlight. Some stories may have hooks that are useful for only one type of occasion. Some stories may have only one really good hook, which is fine if the story is well crafted. Other stories possess so many potential hooks that I call them *universal stories*, meaning they can be used for a wide category of occasions and can hook to a variety of different ideas. What's great about relating our former experiences in the form of first-person stories is that we can choose in advance which hooks of the story we want to reveal, because it's not the story itself that is important; rather, it is the story's stickiness to the key ideas that is important. This means selecting relevant details in advance.

The order in which you reveal the hooks of your story is more art than science. A Hollywood movie can start at the beginning of a day and reveal a progression of events in chronological order until the end of that day. It can also start with the end of the day and work backward through a series of flashbacks. The sequence or order in which you reveal the hooks is not overly important, but I recommend you explore different variations, as sometimes starting at the end or beginning can lead to stronger connections to your other ideas. In terms of the ordering of the hooks, one effective way to enhance stickiness is to adhere to parallel construction. For example, imagine I want to make these three ideas more memorable:

1. Customer care is our goal.
2. Our supply chain should be treated with customer care.
3. Profitability is testimony of our customer care ability.

I can relate a story that illustrates these ideas in any order I choose, so long as the hooks revealed through the storytelling are presented in the same sequence as these three points. Parallel construction should follow sequence, because it is easy for the brain. And easy usually confers more stickiness.

## Dialogue

I know people who relate solid-gold stories without ever mentioning what someone in the story said. When they do this they tend to relate the story in the past tense, as something that already happened. Although relating a prior personal event in this manner can instruct and can even reveal hooks you want to use to stick to other ideas, using dialogue significantly enhances a story's stickiness.

Dialogue means that someone in your story speaks. When someone speaks in a story, the story becomes more personal. If I were relating a story about a former manager, I need to make sure that at some point she speaks, meaning I have to tell you what she said. For instance, if I'm telling a story about how I blew it at a meeting one time in my early career, I might say something like, "She pulled me aside and hissed, 'You will definitely see this on your performance review.'" Literally repeating what my former manager said, even if it is just a truthful facsimile or approximation of her words, causes additional brain regions in my listeners' brains to light up. Fundamentally, not only does dialogue personalize the story more, but also the dialogue itself co-opts more brain-processing functions in the listeners' brains, meaning they have to devote more attention to what I am saying. And more attention is a good thing.

In addition to personalizing the story and lighting up more brain regions, dialogue lends itself to relating a former experience as if it is happening at the moment I'm telling the story. This time-shift aspect of dialogue is important. A story is more vividly experienced if the listener experiences it as if it were currently happening. We reviewed this idea in chapter 3 on the central movie. Dialogue is an effective tool for helping the listener see prior actions as continuing to happen or happening in the present, which strengthens listener's attention to want to act on this information in the future.

As with details, not all dialogue is important, and you need to consider which parts reinforce which hooks. In fact, a hook may be revealed with dialogue, which can make it more memorable, since the brain is activated more fully when listening to this portion of the story. Scrub the dialogue of your story for the best bits, just as you would do with details.

## Drama

Is your story a cautionary tale? Is its purpose to inspire? Is it a story about victory under pressure? Do you want to convey the merits of perseverance? Will it help reinforce maintenance of ethical behavior? Is it a story that starts out sad and ends jubilantly? The drama or dramatic arc of a story underpins its power.

Carlo Gozzi, a noted Italian playwright of the sixteenth century, proposed the idea that there were thirty-six plots available to a writer, each corresponding to a distinct emotion. Two centuries later, the French writer Georges Polti updated this idea, elaborating upon the dramatic plots with titles such as "falling prey to cruelty," "sacrificing for an ideal," and "fatal imprudence." In the late twentieth century these dramatic categories became more process oriented. Blake Snyder described the ten screenplay ideas and earned an admiring following.[26]

Certainly others, too, have advocated this or that schematic for considering drama, and I invite you to peruse their ideas as a method to enhance your own skill at storytelling. I have developed a baker's dozen of situations leaders commonly encounter that beg for stories. This is simply a starter list; there are plenty of other categories.

Identity: Who am I?
Purpose: Why are we here?
Foresight: Where are we going? How will we get there?
Inspiration: How do we keep hope and passion alive?
Negotiation: Why are we changing? How will it affect us?
Conflict negotiation: How do we deal with conflict?
Operating methods: What processes or methods should we use?
Problem solving: How will we figure this out?
Collaboration: How will we work together?
Key messages: Why is this message of particular importance?
Culture: What makes us special? How are we different?
Values: What are our guiding principles? Do we live by them?

Each of these call for stories with enough drama to help instruct, inspire, or invite us to consider our thoughts about their merits.

# Summary

Metaphors and stories are the powerhouses of the symbolic channel. They are natural features of all our communication, and from the neurological evidence available, they appear to work even when other parts of mental functioning are compromised. The most fundamental idea research stresses is not to treat these components as literary adornment or inconsequential artifacts of how humans think, reason, communicate, and behave.

Metaphors organize our thinking, shape our judgments, and structure our communication. You can skate by on casual usage, or you can improve your leadership communication by becoming more thoughtful and deliberate with your metaphorical expressions. There are three methods of metaphor development: steal, prototype, and invent. Each of these requires different degrees of deliberation. Although you may worry that trying out a deliberate metaphorical expression may fail, keep in mind that casual metaphorical expressions can fail as well, so don't worry. In fact, in everyday, ordinary conversation about substantial topics, pausing to hunt for the right metaphor as you speak can appear either like you are being thoughtful or that you don't understand what you are talking about very well. Crafting your metaphors for important topics ahead of time should at least reduce the latter appearance.

We make sense of the world through stories. Indeed, a central movie is a large, time-expanded, coherent story that knits our lives together to provide individual and collective meaning. Considering stories only as casual illustrations to make a point undervalues this communication gold mine. When using stories, remember to include the details, dialogue, and drama. Details provide atmosphere, create hooks, and sequence the comparison between the story and the points you want to make. Dialogue personalizes your story and affects its relevance for the future in terms of the verb tense you use in the telling. And drama involves selecting the overall dramatic tone for the story as applied to a specific audience. Drama challenges the storyteller and the audience to consider their own convictions and often make difficult choices.

One of the political masters of storytelling in United States history was Abraham Lincoln, whose abilities were honed over a lifetime of practice. Doris Kearns Goodwin references Lincoln's oratorical skills throughout her book *Team of Rivals*. In particular, she writes, "Lincoln's stories provided more than mere amusement. Drawn from his own experiences and the curiosities reported by others, they frequently provided maxims and proverbs that usefully connected to the lives of his listeners. Lincoln possessed an extraordinary ability to convey practical wisdom in the form of humorous tales his listeners would remember and repeat."[27]

I believe we can all tap some of that power by simply practicing our storytelling a little more.

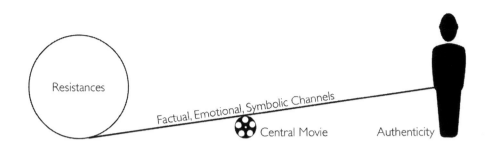

Resistances

Factual, Emotional, Symbolic Channels

Central Movie

Authenticity

# EMOTIONAL CHANNEL

Like it or not, your emotional system is always on. Many of us prefer to think we can make "rational" decisions, meaning decisions based on facts alone, uncontaminated by unreliable emotions, but hopefully by now the information in this book has helped you see the error of this line of thinking. The entire reason-without-emotion construct has been demolished by modern evidence. In fact, experiencing, sorting, and controlling emotions enhance decision making and communication; trying to eliminate them is a futile task.

I recently had a conversation about this with a former army officer. He strongly objected to the idea that humans can't eliminate emotions from their actions. He talked about the hours of difficult training he and his fellow soldiers would go through in order to complete a mission without letting messy feelings get in the way. His mantra was clear—we train, we execute our training, and we complete our mission. Emotions have nothing to do with it.

When I asked him why they trained so hard, he said, "So we could have control over our feelings in very dynamic and sometimes ugly situations."

"Ah, so basically the training you went through helped you identify an emotional state, then put you in a training situation so that you could encounter and experience this emotion and learn how to control it," I said.

"Exactly."

"After this training, how did your team feel?"

"Their confidence was up, they operated better as a unit, and they felt prepared to tackle anything that came up during the mission."

"So basically your unit learned to control unwanted feelings like maybe fear, surprise, or panic, and left them with more positive feelings like confidence and controlled aggression."

"You could say that," he said. I began to see that the gears in his head were churning.

"Is it possible that other groups of people who have to encounter difficult situations, especially ones that might lead to personal harm, might learn to do the same thing? Like fire and rescue personnel, the police, airplane pilots, or emergency room workers?" I asked.

"Of course. I get your point. Emotions aren't eliminated; they are controlled."

"Exactly. Unwanted emotions get controlled, and desirable emotions get promoted. And thank goodness your training was so tough and thorough, because you likely were in situations that caused a lot of potential emotions to erupt."

"I can't talk about that," he said, winking in a conspiratorial manner.

Whenever I have these conversations, it is apparent that people really do understand that emotions don't get eliminated but can be controlled, which is an important aspect of emotional maturity. Having emotions isn't the problem, but dealing with them can be. I marvel in irony that some companies desire passionate talent and then demand that they dispassionately present information to their superiors, rely upon only factual information concerning innovation practices, and manage personnel exclusively through metric-oriented performance reviews.

Emotions are always on. And as the conversation above indicates, learning to deal with strong emotions requires work. As Joseph LeDoux, a noted expert on emotional circuitry, states, "Emotions easily bump mundane events out of awareness, but non-emotional events (like thoughts) do not so easily displace emotions from the mental spotlight."[1]

Our lives are far more influenced by our emotional states than we want to believe, because *we* want to believe *we* are in charge, not our feelings. Kenneth Dodge, professor of psychology and neuroscience at Duke University, goes so far as to conclude, "All information processing is emotional, in that emotion is the energy that drives, organizes, amplifies, and attenuates cognitive activity and in turn is the experience and expression of this activity."[2] LeDoux and others add to Dodge's expression of emotional processing the idea that cognitive and emotional systems work together to help individuals both understand and manage emotions. "The mixing of basic emotions into higher order emotions is typically thought of as a cognitive operation."[3]

Fundamentally, thinking cannot be fully comprehended if emotions are ignored. Neither can communication.

## Emotional States

Different researchers have created different categories and schematics in order to try to reduce a dense and difficult amount of clinical data into understandable chunks. The general agreement among the experts is:

1. The three categories of emotional state are mood, primary emotions, and social emotions.
2. Primary emotions and mood are mixed through cognitive operations to produce social emotions.
3. Emotions can be influenced by our interactions with others.

It's likely that you're not surprised by any of these ideas. An initial reaction to a situation may trip your fear emotion, but your confidence might mix with this initial reaction with the result being concern or apprehension rather than outright terror. This mixing of emotions has been explained in a manner similar to mixing primary colors on a color wheel. Primary colors combine to produce a huge array of shades and hues, which are terms we also often apply to emotional states.

The late Robert Plutchik invested a good deal of his intellectual career exploring this process. He suggested that there are eight primary emotions and that blending them can produce secondary and then even tertiary emotions. For example, joy plus anticipation produces optimism. Anger plus disgust produces contempt.[4] Others use different schematics to discuss the shades of emotions. W. Gerrod Parrott, professor of psychology at Georgetown University, has proposed a tree-like structural organization of emotions. Love as a primary emotion branches into secondary expressions of affection, lust, and longing. And a third branching reveals emotions such as affection, liking, and tenderness.[5] Parrott is currently exploring the idea that basic emotions might be reclassified as ur-emotions.[6] I take Damasio's stance that although feelings and emotions can be discussed clinically as connected but different, they "are so intimately related along a continuous process that we tend to think of them, understandably, as one single thing."[7] It appears that scientists can talk about emotions easily, until asked to define what they are. I will use the ideas of primary emotions, background emotions (mood), and social emotions as a simple classification scheme that is familiar to everyone.

Primary emotions are stimulated by a variety of potential triggers, such as any direct experience, reflecting on your past, empathy, having one of your values violated, even simply assuming the appearance of the emotion, which I will discuss later. The emotions produced by these triggers are processed in both the emotional and cognitive systems, which is why interrupting either processing system or the ability for the two to interact leads to difficulties. This internal processing of emotion is further influenced by our social interactions.

In modern parlance within business circles, two ideas are circulating with deserved popularity. One of these is emotional intelligence, which largely has to do with how individuals manage emotions and emotional states. The ability to detect and manage your own primary emotional reactions and your ongoing mood is paramount to successful management or leadership. The second idea is social intelligence, or how we influence one another, which has a profound effect on just about everything—in particular, our emotional states. As Daniel Goleman puts it, the sum total of all our social interactions in a very direct sense creates who we are.[8]

Moods can be described as prolonged emotional states, and the word is often used by clinicians to describe general emotional outlook. The person who is sad much of the time is depressed. The person who is on a happy high all the time is perhaps regarded as manic. In a more conversational and ordinary sense, though, we use the term *mood* to describe a background feeling that lasts from a few minutes or hours to a day or two. Likely you have had the blues or felt on top of the world for a few hours or perhaps as long as weekend. Neither condition may have persisted, and as the more momentary feelings subside, you return to more of your normal everyday self with emotions spiking or relaxing through a typical course of events.

In this second sense a great deal of literature suggests that mood matters in terms of productivity, creativity, problem solving, resolve, and cooperation. I imagine if I asked you if mood matters when it comes to work performance, you would have no hesitation answering yes. And you'd be right. It does matter. And how leaders handle their moods is as important as how they control their own emotional states. Damasio argues, "One of the many reasons why some people become leaders and others followers, why some command respect and others cower, has little to do with knowledge or skills and a lot to do with how certain physical traits and the manner of a given individual promote certain emotional responses in others."[9] We follow leaders because of the feelings they inspire. And as I have shown in chapter 1, inspiration is always linked to communication. Our internal inspiration is ignited when leaders communicate a central movie worthy of inspiration. We know the movie is inspiring when we become more energized, more galvanized, more passionate about our work.

Goleman and his co-authors Robert Boyatzis and Annie McKee are even more enthusiastic in their conclusions about mood: "Taken as a whole, the message sent by neurological, psychological, and organizational research is startling in its clarity. Emotional leadership is the spark that ignites a company's a performance, creating a bonfire of success or a landscape of ashes. Moods matter that much."[10]

Moods and other emotional states also propagate socially. Have you ever seen a down mood or an up mood sweep across an athletic team? These more temporary mood swings can be interrupted by pep talks from the coach, team members managing their personal feelings and communicating positively to their teammates, and the background support (or dissent) of fans. James Fowler and Nicholas Christakis, both at Harvard, published a provocative study in the

*British Medical Journal* indicating that happiness appears to spread outward as a social contagion as far as three degrees of separation from the initial happy person or group.[11] Christakis and others later revealed similar results with regard to depression, obesity, teamwork, and other social phenomena.[12]

Developing more emotional maturity and influencing the emotional states of groups is at the heart of the emotional intelligence and social intelligence movements. Communication is at the core of these subjects, so let's look at how it works.

## Communicating Emotions

Communicating on the emotional channel requires two broad abilities:

1. In relevant ways that are appropriate to social norms and the situation, leaders must declare their emotional states.
2. In relevant ways that are appropriate to social norms and the situation, leaders must demonstrate empathy for others' emotional states.

This may sound easy, and indeed from a science point of view it is easy to state. From a practical point of view, however, it can be very tough.

Leaders need to declare their emotional states for two reasons. First, it dismisses speculation. The poker-faced, factual, robotic leader is at best hard to pull off and at worst a fiction. We ascribe motivation, emotional character, and intent to machines and robots. Helen Greiner, one of iRobot Corporation's founders, discussed how people named their Roomba robotic vacuum cleaners and even refused to send them back to the manufacturer for machine repairs, preferring specialists to make house calls for their ailing companions.[13] (To imagine we don't ascribe emotions to non-emotive devices defies experience. My guess is that you have cursed a computer, automobile, piece of sports gear, or even a furniture item for its disobedience to your wishes.) Don't allow others to guess your emotional state. They may be wrong, and if they are, they are filling in the blanks and making a movie different from the one you want them to view.

The second reason declaring your emotional state is important is that by stating your own feelings you are likely naming the feelings shared by at least some of your constituents. Those who already share them are reinforced; those who don't either prepare to resist your message (worst-case scenario) or may be influenced to shift their emotional perspective (best-case scenario). The best-case scenario is enhanced when a leader demonstrates relevant empathy.

Demonstrating empathy, in communication terms, means stating the range of emotions that exist in terms of the situation. Leaders must say that they know certain feelings exist for some membership of the group, even if the leader does not share those feelings. Imagine you are about to speak to a team at a quarterly update meeting, and you know that one-third of people in the room are feeling positive about the results and next steps, one-third are ambivalent, and the remaining third are upset and annoyed by the results and disagree with the next steps. The worst thing a leader can do, in terms of the emotional channel, is ignore the group's feelings and show no emotional empathy.

The second worst thing a leader can do is pander to only one of the three groups. For example, if you simply say, "I know you are excited by our results and look forward to our next steps," you have reached only one-third of the group and likely created an increase in emotional resistance to your message for the other two-thirds. It is possible that some of the third who share your emotions are put off by your insensitivity to the emotions of the other two-thirds. If you were to also say, "I know you are frustrated by what is happening and our results are not up to your liking, but here's what we are going to do anyway," you really haven't shown empathy to the upset third, and the other two groups are wondering why they are left out of the equation.

The best thing you can do is to acknowledge and demonstrate empathy for each of the three groups and then make your case for why the mood should shift. Research conducted on my three-channel model has shown that emotional resistance to your message is among the most difficult resistances to overcome. Demonstrating empathy may not cure the resistance of your constituents, but ignoring their feelings definitely makes the situation worse.

Emphasizing your emotional states can take on a wide range of behavior. I've watched Steve Ballmer, CEO of Microsoft, jump around on stage in an enthusiastic emotional display in front of thousands, shouting his "I love this company!" mantra for ten minutes to great applause. I've also seen Roy Vallee, executive chief of the board for Avnet, inspire a group during difficult times with a less theatric, highly effective, genuinely confident and authentic display of emotional declaration and empathy. We can conflate apparent enthusiasm for emotional intelligence or more quiet leadership with a lack of emotional energy. John Mayer is a psychologist at the University of New Hampshire and a thought leader in the emotional intelligence arena. He suggests, "A person high in emotional intelligence may be realistic rather than optimistic and insecure rather than confident. Conversely, a person may be highly self-confident and optimistic but lack emotional intelligence. The danger lies in assuming that because a person is optimistic or confident, he or she is also emotionally intelligent, when, in fact, the presence of those traits will tell you nothing of the sort."[14]

A leader reveals emotional intelligence by her willingness and ability to declare personal emotional states and demonstrate genuine empathy for others' emotional states. Using these two aspects of emotional channel communication can influence the maintenance of emotional states, like keeping inspiration and hope alive. It can also influence a change in emotional states, such as converting cynicism, routing apprehension, or overturning feelings of failure. "Scholars of interpersonal communication tell us that openness invites openness; disclosure, disclosure. Self-disclosure can accelerate our sense of intimacy in a relationship."[15]

Emotional declarations are important. The ability to pick up on mood and demonstrate empathy is important as well. Better leaders are able to detect moods and influence changes in the mood of individuals and groups. There is power in literally naming the emotional states you are experiencing as a leader, as well as naming the feelings you know exist within your constituent group. Individuals who are able to literally put their feelings into words gain greater control of those feelings and reduce their impact.[16] In a very similar sense, if a leader has accurately detected the variety of feelings in a group and states them, this labeling effect can pass from leader to follower. This precise labeling of feelings is a significant component of empathy through communication. It increases your authenticity and appeal with the group and grants them a moment of greater emotional control over the feelings of the moment.

You can see evidence of this even when leaders are trying to describe a wide range of feelings to a diverse constituency. Havel's speech that I discussed in chapter 3 was powerful in terms of labeling feelings. He spoke during a major turning point in history, addressing a wide range of emotions as you might imagine. At the time of the speech conditions were dire, the mood gloomy, and Havel needed to address a huge backload of emotional disappointment. Reading just the first half dozen paragraphs of his speech reveals the following words he used that refer to or describe different emotional states:

bleak, astonished, surprise, anticipate, joyful, doubt, distress, pleasant, guilt, nervous, hope, fear, impatience, disappointment, malice, suspicion, shock, embarrassment, uncertainty

John F. Kennedy's inaugural address memorializes a different turning point in history in the United States. In just the first third of his speech he refers to a variety of emotional states, often in a more stylized symbolic manner that was more appropriate for that period in history. Some of the more direct emotional states he referred to are:

celebration, renewal, generosity, hardship, bitter, tempered, hope, foolish, misery, hostility, aggressive, temptation, weakness, sincerity, fear

It may be easy to argue that these examples from political leadership are loaded with emotional phrases because the audiences were huge and because political persuasion requires emotional artistry. My research shows that when business leaders are at their best, they are direct and unambiguous in both declaring their emotional states to their constituents and accurately portraying the variety of emotional moods. The need for these emotional declarations and demonstrations of empathy are important in all of life's aspects, whether attending a meeting, supporting a political rally, talking over troubles with your friends or relatives, or encouraging your children to do their best.

Proximity and contact aid mood detection. Group size and geographic dispersion offer significant challenges for mood detection. This means it's harder for leaders to detect constituent moods and vice versa. We see others' faces, hear voice tones, observe body language, and see how others react to our faces, tones, and body language. But when leaders have dispersed constituencies, these conduits of emotional information are at best constrained with a communication tourniquet and at worst severed entirely. We simply have a far more difficult time having access to vital emotional information when we don't often see and hear one another.

This leads to three conditions. First we construct our current understanding of another's emotional state based upon prior encounters. If those encounters are many and significantly varied, we have a decent chance at extrapolating how others might be feeling based on fewer nonverbal clues. Call a family member or a co-worker you know well, and just vocal tone alone can help you detect what likely is occurring emotionally. The second condition creates more uncertainty and potential for miscommunicating. We extrapolate how others might be feeling when we have a sparse database of prior experience from a more general database of human understanding. The problem is that our global, generalized database of how most people feel may be way off in terms of a specific individual or small group. The third condition is the worst. We don't have much of a means to know what others are feeling, and therefore we ignore this factor or convince ourselves that others' feelings are irrelevant. This is business, after all; why do I care how others feel? They should just do the job I tell them to do.

Researchers have known for a long time that nonverbal cues play a huge role in conveying emotional signals. Individuals who are more nonverbally expressive are seen as better communicators and are more likable. Those who display a larger range of expressions are viewed as more self-confident and garner larger social networks than others. It even goes further. Some researchers put three strangers in a room together and asked them not to speak to one another. What the researchers wanted to know is how well strangers could pick up on mood simply based on nonverbal information. The strangers who demonstrated a greater range of nonverbal cues, even without trying or being asked to try, were able to transmit their mood to the other two with far more accuracy than those who exhibited fewer or more subdued nonverbal cues.[17]

Those who are better at communicating their emotional states are using nonverbal visual cues in a more effective manner than others and are having a more significant effect on the mood of the group. This means these individuals are likely the better regulators of both information and mood than others.

# Nonverbal Attributes of Emotional Communication

"Mirror neurons will do for psychology what DNA did for biology," V. S. Ramachandran has said.[18] Mirror neurons are part of our neurological equipment. They engage or fire when we perform an action, like reaching for a mouse or keyboard. They also engage when we see someone else reach for a mouse or a keyboard. Ramachandran is a neuroscientist and director of the Center for Brain and Cognition in conjunction with the University of California, San Diego. In a TED talk of November 2009 he described this mirroring action as if one person were adopting a virtual reality simulation of what they saw another person do.[19] He claimed the varieties of functions that different types of mirror neurons have are an essential part of empathy's neural circuitry. He even speculated that these mirror neurons accelerate the transmission of culture.

If someone smiles at you, you have an increased tendency to smile back, because your mind automatically mirrors the movement. Part of this mirror neuron system identifies emotional status based upon the movements observed. We see a smile and we think *happy, pleased, in a state of uplifted mood.* We see tears and we think *unhappy, hurt, in a state of depressed mood.* It should come as no surprise that our nonverbal cues help inform the meaning of our language. "How we understand what is being said is not strictly a function of the words we hear, but the combination of the words, tone accompanying the words, and the visual cues of the speaker. Eliminate the source of any of these cues and the meaning can change," according to Jeremy Skipper and his colleagues.[20]

Mirror neurons help us empathize by mentally replicating gestures we see in others' faces, body movements, and their tone of voice. These cues are part and parcel of how we construct meaning. Another part of our brains works in tandem with mirror neurons to understand the replicated emotions in the social context in which they occur. This system, known as the mentalizing system, adds to the observed verbal behavior the social context information that accompanies the communication. A very recent series of interesting experiments performed by Robert Spunt and Matthew Lieberman at UCLA have shown there is a sequence to mirroring and mentalizing systems.[21] The mirroring system fires first and then informs the mentalizing system. This means the gestures that accompany our emotional states hit our brains first and then assist our more cognitive abilities to understand the emotion they are witnessing.

You may not care too much about the neuroscience of how mirroring, mentalizing, and meaning apply to the emotional channel, but you do know from experience that these things count. Michael Tomasello is co-director of the Max Planck Institute for Evolutionary Theory and one of the foremost scientists studying gesture origins. As an authority on how human gesture-oriented communication preceded our development of structured vocal communication, Tomasello makes a strong case that pointing and pantomiming emerged prior to vocal communication. Gestures developed as a means for humans to indicate intentions and were the earliest forms of cooperative communication. And he asserts that conventional communication is only possible when individuals possess these natural gestures that convey shared intentions and have the ability to learn these conventions and constructs.[22] His research is supported by a variety of other well-established facts about gestures. For example, blind babies gesture from birth. Even though they have never seen someone else gesture, pointing and pantomiming gestures accompany babies' vocalizations.

Deaf babies who begin learning sign language at the same age as hearing babies learn to speak will engage in what Laura Ann Petito calls "hand babbling."[23] This means that the gestures babies use as they are learning to sign are clumsy, often funny attempts at replicating the signs they are learning, just like hearing babies learning to speak. Petito's research shows that deaf individuals store language in phonetic and syllabic units the same way as sighted people do. They don't carry around little pictures in their heads. Regardless if you learn the American, French, or English versions of sign language, your brain learns it using the same processing components that people learning oral speech use. And to connect this to the other components of our model, deaf people employ metaphor, visual alliteration, and other symbolic channel tools in their communication.

A final nod to the innateness of gestures is marvelously portrayed in Margalit Fox's book, *Talking Hands*. The inhabitants of Al-Sayyid, an isolated Bedouin village in the Negev desert, close to the communities of Beersheba and Hura, independently developed a sign language used by all members of the community and only recently decoded by linguists. The reason everyone there uses this language is because roughly 30 percent of the inhabitants are born deaf. However, the gestural structure of the language follows other sign languages, even though the linguists had to learn the conventions of this unique language.[24]

Here's the short version of all this science: gestures matter, especially on the emotional channel. Gestures, tonal qualities, and even slight facial expressions convey emotion as effectively as the words we use when we say how we feel. In fact, researchers will tell you that your words may lie about your feelings but your body does not. Ask someone how they feel, and if they answer with a sighing tone and slumping shoulders, "Fine," which part of the communication do you believe?

Paul Ekman is a noted authority on gestures and their interplay with spoken communication. He has studied in depth the thousands of subtle facial expressions that occur as a person speaks, and he has a highly developed ability to detect lying. Lying is a complex subject that incorporates both cognition and emotion, but even professional liars can be caught when the natural gestures that accompany typical emotional states are absent during the lie. This means a person feigns a particular emotion but fails to accompany the appropriate gesture with the fake emotion. This creates an incongruity between these two communication sources. Even if we pick up on the incongruity unconsciously, our brains alert our consciousness with a nagging feeling of uncertainty. For experts like Ekman, who are trained to look for even fleeting gestures often referred to as microexpressions, even small incongruities tell large stories.

## Four Kinds of Gestures

All the body movements, facial expressions, and tonal qualities that people use can be collected into one bag and labeled as *gestures*. Within the emotional channel, gestures can be classified into four groups: emblematic, illustrative, regulatory, and affective.

Make the letter "L" with your right hand and hold it against your forehead, and the world knows you are signaling "Loser!" Extend your arm straight in front of your torso, hand pointing up, and nearly everyone sees that as a sign for stop. Waving hello or good-bye is one of the first *emblematic* gestures we learn as children, and we soon learn the gesture itself is sufficient. Vocal silence isn't communication silence. Think about the emblematic gestures that accompany these communications:

- Quiet!
- Call me
- Peace
- Bring me the check
- Ok
- You first
- My lips are sealed
- Victory
- They went that away
- Yes
- No
- I don't know
- I don't care

You get the picture, er, gesture. Emblematic gestures are used around the world, and the typical advice of being wary of their use is useful. You have heard and perhaps experienced how one gesture means different things in different parts of the world. My advice is to learn the conventions wherever you live. Trying to avoid the use of gestures limits your communication ability and is futile anyway.

*Illustrative* gestures are a very robust part of our everyday speech. These are gestures that accompany a word, phrase, idea, or action and accent or illustrate what you are saying. For example, if I say we are going to review three things in this meeting today and hold up three fingers, I've amplified the idea of "three." Sometimes this counting of three things is illustrated by literally counting them off *one, two, three* by holding up one, two, and three fingers. More often we tap the appropriate number of digits with one hand onto the fingers or palm of our other hand as we speak.

If I am explaining something to you that I am assured you understand, I may punctuate my speech with the phrase, "You know what I mean?" This phrase is often accompanied with raised eyebrows and/or a head nod or tilt. These same facial gestures can accompany other phrases or meanings and accent the context in several different ways. Lip pursing, smiles, and frowns also accent ideas or phrases.

Other illustrative gestures indicate movements over time or direction. If we say we are going up in sales, our gestures go up. Same for down. Sometimes we might even say our sales progress has been a rollercoaster and our hands wave up and down as we speak, illustrating the idea. We point to the past, present, and future as we speak. When we talk about when our children were young, we sometimes use our hands to show how tall they were then. If I say something like, "I want this to stop right now!" I might accompany that expression with a dramatic arm and hand gesture that points or chops downward toward my feet, indicating the present. Humans use a rich, sometimes inventive repertoire of illustrative gestures to further illustrate or accent our communication. Many of these accompany our communication in the moment, without thought.

*Regulatory* gestures depict the rhythm, pacing, or tempo of discourse. They can be body movements or facial expressions that Ekman refers to as baton-accents or baton-underliners.[25] *Baton* in this sense refers to the pointer an orchestral conductor uses when keeping time and tempo. Most of our regulatory gestures are relatively rough, sporadic, and underdeveloped. In the worst case they are regarded as simple arm flapping. Which is why you are often instructed to keep your hands at your side, to control these sporadic and underdeveloped gestures. Too many presentation skills instructors give this advice, which I consider useful only as a last resort. As I will soon discuss, any category of gesture can be helpful if you learn to use it well. Being told not to use a particular gesture, without substituting a different gesture or pose, more often than not limits your communication ability.

The fourth category of gestures (can you imagine I am holding up four fingers?) is *affective*. These are the gestures of the head, neck, and face that accompany a suite of emotions that are universally expressed. Some researchers do not single out these gestures as a separate category, but consider different facial movements as illustrative, regulatory, or emblematic. I agree with this classification. I separate the "above-the-neck" into a separate category simply for ease of comment. Movement of our lips, eyebrows, head can accompany illustrative gestures or serve as emblematic gestures, but primarily they convey affect or feeling.

More than half the emotional information we obtain from gestures is conveyed above the neck and via vocal tone. Much of the facial information is also difficult or impossible to control, which is why maintaining a poker face can be a challenge, except for some individuals who possess rare neurological conditions. And a high portion of emotional information conveyed by nonverbal means comes through tonal qualities like pitch and rate of speech. The two most regular mistakes managers make in terms of affective gestures is trying way too hard to control them (poker face) or trying way too hard to fake them (feigning feeling). Both of these result in constituents working too hard to understand the real emotion behind the communication and when we work hard, we fill in the blanks.

Communication congruity is often experienced as a gut check. When the communicated ideas are supported by what we see (gestures) and hear (voice intonations) on the emotional channel, our emotional brains do not alert our other systems that anything is amiss. We literally get a feeling in our body that something isn't right (likely our mirror neurons are involved with the inconsistency between words and gestures). Hiding or faking gestures creates incongruity, meaning a communicator is saying one thing in words and something different in gesture. When this happens constituents' emotional systems go on congruity alert. We start filling in the blanks in an attempt to reconcile the disparate movies being presented. This can results in constituents discounting the communication, disbelieving the communication, or disrupting the communication by either ignoring or challenging the communicator. Repeated episodes of a leader hiding or feigning leads most people to down-tick the authenticity or credibility of the communicator, which decreases the leader's effectiveness, increases constituents' congeniality bias, and kicks in the four fatal assumptions.

Among the primary reasons that all communication other than face-to-face is more difficult is because of the lack of visual or vocal tone information. At least in telephone conversations we have the opportunity to detect and assess tonal qualities. Emoticons were not invented by schoolchildren as mere visual adornment to written messages. They were invented as pictographic substitutes to satisfy the cravings of the emotional system for information. While their usage evokes both criticism and applause, they were invented, and are used, to solve a problem.

As a leader you must use your gestures well. My recommendations for gestures are as follows:

- Study your natural repertoire of gestures.
- Amplify those that are working.
- Substitute those that don't work with something else.
- Find methods for conveying emotional information when you are not face-to-face.
- Stop annoying gestures if possible (substitution is often more feasible than elimination).

There are two activities I strongly recommend for studying your use of gestures. The first is to use a confederate who is sensitive to or trained in the area of gestures and who can observe you in meetings and presentations. This confederate can take notes on your use and range of especially illustrative and affective gestures. Having that person video-record you during group meetings or presentations for the purposes of providing feedback is strongly recommended as a second activity. Expanding and controlling your range of gestures, facial expressions, and vocal intonations requires feedback, and video-recording is a terrific method.

## Thumbs-Up to Positive Emotions

"The states of minds of others—their intentions, beliefs, attitudes, and emotions—predispose an individual to behave in a certain way. The ability to anticipate the behavior of others is dependent upon the ability to understand other minds."[26] Siegel references the substantial body of knowledge on how we understand the interior conditions of another person, like their mood, intentions, or motivations by correlating body signals with words. As we observe the body signals conforming to the words, our congruity needs are satisfied. As congruity is satisfied, we begin forecasting where the emotional tone is leading. Humor often comes from the novelty of being led down a road through intonation, body language, and word to a particular conclusion and then being surprised by an unanticipated twist.

Leaders are expected not only to maintain congruity but also to project optimism in the form of positive emotions. There are plenty of good reasons for this. Stimulating a positive mood improves performance, enhances a person's ability to remember and evaluate ideas, promotes bolder strategic considerations, encourages initiative, and enhances lateral thinking.[27] Negative emotions or moods strongly tend toward the opposite. Constituents expect both confidence and a positive view of the future from leaders. Feigning confidence or falsely pantomiming a positive image undermines credibility due to incongruence and leads to dampened emotions and increased resistance to the leader's communication.

The effects of positive emotions are well documented, and recent research has indicated that expressions commonly linked to positive or negative emotional states can have long-term effects on the mood of others. Gestures are so entwined with emotional states that they can as powerfully affect positive and negative moods. Giving your constituents a genuine smile or thumbs-up can illicit as long-lasting a positive mood as a pep talk. In fact, positive emotions literally increase a person's visual field of view—we literally open our eyes to more information, which has linkages to the same cognitive functions of opening our minds to more possibilities.[28]

# Summary

The most important parts of the emotional channel in a leader's role are declarations of personal emotional states and demonstrations of empathy for others' emotional states. Ignore either of these, and you can expect emotional resistance to your communication to increase. "Thinking cannot be fully comprehended if emotions and motivations are ignored," LeDoux reminds us.[29]

The emotional channel is enhanced or diminished when constituents are able to view gestures or hear vocal intonations that accompany words. Although we generally know this is true from experience, we regularly forget its importance, especially in today's world, where an abundance of communication is relegated to emails, blogs, and tweets. You can easily improve the effectiveness of your communication by deliberately including direct statements of feeling and mood in your written communications. While this might be challenging for day-to-day email exchanges, most written communications, such as newsletters, blogs, or other internal communications, can be enhanced by attending to labeling your emotions well.

Our feelings and mood are entwined with all of our other cognitive functions and affect everything we do. Relying upon others to "fill in the blanks" because you disregard attending to this channel imperils your leadership effectiveness. Congeniality bias is often difficult to overcome when long-term beliefs have been reinforced by long-term emotional experiences. Affecting a change in congeniality bias requires a sophisticated and effective use of the emotional channel. Maintaining congeniality bias (keeping people inspired about your central movie) also requires effective emotional channel use.

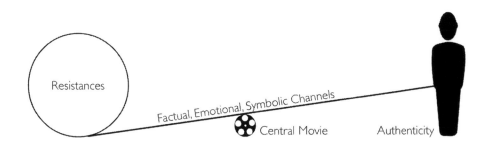

Resistances

Factual, Emotional, Symbolic Channels

Central Movie

Authenticity

# FACTUAL CHANNEL

We swim in an increasingly extensive ocean of information. We look for, revel in, misuse, overuse, and rely upon factual information to organize and make sense of our lives. Facts save lives. Facts fool others. Facts help us choose which menu item to order at a restaurant. Facts help us understand the health of our bodies and our businesses. Some people would rather continue to believe a fantasy than face the facts. Some people experience numerical facts almost like music; they literally enjoy the play and interplay of numbers. Others develop great skill at manipulating facts and know how to distort information toward their own ends. Gossip, what some scientists refer to as social grooming through communication, in its essence is conveying new, hopefully novel bits of information about the interactions of people we know and the general state of affairs.

Facebook, Twitter, and Google+ are parts of a worldwide collage of people posting facts, laughing at facts, disputing one another over the facts, and asserting judgments about facts. When you "like" one of these posts on Facebook, it means you support a point of view, ratify an opinion, or simply enjoy the information. When you quarrel with the post, you present different information, which leads to different conclusions. Some judgments about the facts come down to personal preference, such as the cross-town rivalry we have in Cincinnati as to who is the best chili purveyor, Gold-Star or Skyline. Proponents of both sides of the argument will cite a variety of factual reasons for their preference, argue over the quality of each other's "facts," and even create taste-test competitions to prove their conclusions.

The age-old saying "the facts speak for themselves" is misleading, which should not surprise you. Facts rarely, if ever, speak for themselves. Every individual, from a mother recounting to her child the reasons why broccoli is good for his health to CEOs reminding constituents that pruning the ranks is good for the health of the organization, selects information and arrays this information in the form of a logical conclusion. The individual facts do not speak for themselves. The communicator assembles information, opinions, numbers, statistics, assertions, and data of infinite variety on a selective basis and links these in a chain of reasoning for others to consider. Facts are a powerful part of three-channel leverage, but if you leave them unattached to the emotional and symbolic channels, you will find others using your facts to create a movie that is totally different from the one you are trying to convey.

We use a wide range of factual quality, from what seems to be purely emotional preference to highly scrutinized statistical data to inform our decisions. And our brains have two different logical systems that often act independently to assess factual information and form conclusions. Dean Buonomano, professor of neurobiology and psychology at UCLA, labels them the automatic and reflective logical systems.[1] Nobel laureate Daniel Kahneman, in *Thinking, Fast and Slow*, his delightful review of his decades of hard-won research, refers to them as System 1 and System 2.[2] He does this because he asserts that terms like *System 1* and *2* are easier to remember than *automatic* and *reflective logical systems*.

I prefer simplicity as well but will use the terms *automatic* and *analytic*. The automatic logical system is always on. The analytic system has to be prompted into action. A lot of everyday activity can be handled by the automatic system. When it comes to making an informed decision, like which sofa to purchase or whether or not to acquire another company, the analytic system is usually employed. I say "usually" because there are plenty of times when small- or large-scale decisions are made based upon automatic rather than analytic thinking.

An extensive body of knowledge exists about how our automatic system works, its biases, its sometimes faulty logic. It can dominate our thinking by allowing us to consider and answer easy questions that have "good or bad" or "yes or no" qualities as a substitute for more difficult to answer questions that have to factor several variables and presents answers in statistical shades of gray.

The following table is a list of a very few of the differences between the automatic and analytic factual systems that I see as having the most impact in terms of factual channel communication.

| Automatic | Analytic |
| --- | --- |
| Rapid | Slow |
| Unconscious | Conscious |
| Pattern recognition from experience | Analysis of experience to refine patterns |
| Buggy | Less buggy |
| Gullible, biased toward belief, always working | Unbelieving, biased toward doubt, often lazy |
| Conclusions first, arguments second | Arguments first, conclusions second |
| Links past, present, future together; holds your current "worldview" | Updates worldview through counterfactual thinking, scenario analysis, updating automatic system with more informed information |
| Looks for a single cause | Evaluates alternative causes |

Despite what we like to think about ourselves, the automatic system plays a majority role in what we think and do. The analytic system takes over when a situation becomes more difficult or challenging. And generally this works pretty well, because it efficiently balances two parts of our logical or factual channel systems to sort workloads and attend to them in optimized ways. The automatic system's bias toward fast, pattern-recognition interpretations of what is happening generally works well. For most of what life presents, it provides accurate interpretations and allows us to generate pretty good short-term predictions of what will happen next. By and large pattern recognition works pretty well, and as we build up expert pattern recognition, meaning when our competence in a given arena increases and we have experienced and dealt with a high number of problems in a field of expertise, our pattern-recognition abilities become more valued. Do you want experienced people working with you? Of course. And the more expertise they have, the more we want them (and often the more they can charge for their expertise).

When things get tougher the analytic system kicks in, and it generally overrides the automatic system once employed. The automatic system's worldviews and belief systems can be changed over time with the analytic system's help, but there are plenty of times when the automatic system's faulty logic reinforces congeniality bias rather than allows deeply held beliefs or assumptions to alter. And when the beliefs are deep enough, congeniality bias prevents us from considering evidence to the contrary. This is why facts alone cannot persuade or inspire those who are already predisposed against your communication. But simple emotional appeals or strong symbolism, like a powerful story, cannot overcome congeniality bias alone either. It takes all three channels, working together, to leverage this resistance.

We all have been guilty of selecting only data that reinforce our viewpoint. And even if you are the rare individual who has never distorted, maligned, misrepresented, or otherwise mangled information so that you could get your way, you probably have had someone do it to you. As Brooks Jackson and Kathleen Hall Jamieson vigorously demonstrate in their book *UnSpun: Finding Facts in a World of Disinformation,* "Not only are we surrounded by commercial and political pitchmen who are trying their best to pull the wool over our eyes, but also our own brains betray us in ways that psychologists are struggling to understand."[3]

Let's look at some of the ways we intentionally and unintentionally fool ourselves, and each other, with data. Consider this particular situation. You purchase an ice-cream cone for your child on a hot summer day as a treat for being well-behaved under sweaty conditions. The ice-cream cone costs $1.10. The ice cream is $1.00 more than the cone. How much does the ice cream cost? Answer quickly before reading ahead.

For many people the immediate answer that their automatic system supplies is $1.00. This is one of the buggy aspects of the automatic system. It approximates, and usually the approximations are okay. But the automatic system defers nearly all calculations to the analytic system, which is lazy and sometimes has to be persuaded to engage and has to be trained on how to solve the problem. For the above problem, if you derived the right answer, which is $1.05, your analytic system had to create a mathematical equation (which only a few would do) or use successive approximations to derive an answer that can be easily verified (which is what you probably did if you got the right answer). This is the only answer that satisfies the condition that the ice cream is $1.00 more than the cone when the total adds to $1.10.

There are many examples of this type of automatic system faultiness, to which we often succumb, both when presenting or absorbing data presented to us. There are times when the leader's logic falls prey to this automatic system and the illogic may gain more momentum, since not only do our own automatic systems accept a wrong answer, but also our bias is reinforced by an authority figure. Other times the leader's logic is not faulty, which makes the communication fraudulent. This happens when the leader hopes the automatic system's faultiness will pass scrutiny.

Facts we know do not always come to mind when we need them. Daniel Kahneman, in his book *Thinking, Fast and Slow*, discusses many original and groundbreaking experiments that reveal the basic cognitive frailties of our automatic system. In one experiment, when groups were asked to guess the number of murders committed in one year in the state of Michigan, they guessed lower rates than when asked to guess the number of murders committed in one year in the city of Detroit.[4] This demonstrates the cognitive frailty called *availability bias*. When we are asked a general question, our automatic systems quickly bring into consciousness that information which is most readily and easily accessible in order to form an answer. If the answer seems coherent and reasonable to us, we stop considering the question and believe we have the answer. It is only when we are shown additional data that we should have considered that we chuckle to ourselves, or get a little irritated, and realize if we had thought a moment longer, we would have derived the correct answer. This thinking a moment longer is the analytic system kicking in. I believe this is part of whatever success the Campbell Soup Company has had with their "I could have had a V8!" advertising initiative. They are helping you expand your availability bias to include their drink.

We train our analytical systems through education and practice, but even these can be fooled or tricked at times simply because our brains are far better at pattern recognition and remembering simple rules than conducting statistical analysis. One example of this showcases how the automatic system looks for and establishes causality in data, even when none exists. For example, imagine you work in the pediatric ward of a hospital and six babies in a row are delivered over the course of one evening. Which of the following delivery patterns do you think is more likely to happen?

Boy Boy Boy Girl Girl Girl
Girl Girl Girl Girl Girl Girl
Boy Girl Boy Boy Girl Boy

I'll go out on a limb and say you probably guessed the third choice as most likely. Even if you didn't, you probably rejected the second choice as way against the odds. The fact is that any one birth is totally independent of any other. The ratio of boy and girl births is close enough to fifty-fifty that birth clusters are like coin tosses. Getting three heads in a row doesn't have anything to do with the fourth toss. That toss has a fifty-fifty chance of coming up heads or tails, which is the same for the next birth being a boy or girl. But our automatic system wants to see *causality* and therefore will make up a story that choice number three above appears more random, so that it fits more easily to our coin toss understanding.

Here's one final example. I heard this in a TED conference presentation by Peter Donnelly, professor of statistical science at Oxford and director of the Wellcome Trust Centre for Human Genetics.[5] (He joked that a statistician is a person who loves figures but doesn't have the interpersonal skills to become an accountant.) Imagine you are flipping coins and trying to work out if one sequence of flips will occur more often than another. The first sequence you are interested is heads-tails-tails, or HTT. The second sequence is heads-tails-heads, or HTH. Based on these two sequences, which of the following would you choose to be the right answer?

1. HTT sequence, on average, occurs more frequently.
2. Both HTT and HTH occur at the same frequency.
3. HTH sequence, on average, occurs more frequently.

If you guessed answer number two, you are in great company with nearly all individuals, including skilled mathematicians. Generally speaking we know that the odds of either heads or tails occurring in a single fair coin toss are fifty-fifty. And the brilliant company you are in (which includes me when I first guessed) is brilliantly incorrect. The right answer is number one, HTT. This is a terrific example of how the automatic system answers an easy question instead of analyzing a harder one.

The easy question is answering the fifty-fifty coin toss question. The harder question is the original one, which asked you to consider a *sequence* of three tosses compared to a different *sequence* of three tosses. The answer to this question has nothing to do with the odds of a single coin toss, but our automatic system grabbed an easy question to answer and was too lazy, or perhaps inexpert, to answer the real question. I will provide an illustration about how the answer works a little later on, as part of my "facts for the factual channel."

These three examples of availability bias, seeking causality, and answering easy questions first and sticking with them if they are satisfying are examples of some of the difficulties of the automatic and analytic systems. The reason this is important is because as a leader you fall prey to these same kludgy brain mistakes as much as anyone else. You need to become better versed at dealing with the facts in your own mind. And, secondly, you need to ensure that your communication doesn't cause your constituents' biases to engage and lead everyone down a happy, easy, seemingly causal but incorrect path. (*Kludge* is a coined word, evidently first introduced by computer specialist Jackson Granholm as a spin on the German word *klug*, meaning smart.[6] *Kludge* and *kludgy* mean "not so smart" in the sense that sometimes we assemble computer systems and software from bits and pieces we have created before, and the whole mess works some of the time but not all the time. Kind of like our brains.)

Not all facts are numbers in the sense of measurements, calculations, or analyses. Some facts are simple assertions. We assert that customers are our only focus, that we are the best company to work for, and that our products and services are the best, even when proving any of these statements exactly and precisely might be a bit tricky. Other assertions that help us see the logic in a train of thought have to do with past decisions. For example, we refer to how we took the right-hand fork in the road two years ago—not to reopen the data analysis of that decision, but simply to remind people of historic events that provide a reason to understand the current information.

Some facts are simply raw data. Others are derived data from analysis. Some facts compete with one another for dominance in decision making. At the end of the day, leaders must assemble raw data, derived data, assertions, and other forms of "facts" and assemble them into logical stories that showcase their thinking. Most decisions made by leaders are based upon conflicting sets of information, insufficient or questionable data input, or best guesses based upon expertise. Leaders then communicate these decisions to plenty of critics who believe their own factual information is superior.

# Communicating the Facts

The communication of facts is confounded by or enhanced through two equally powerful aspects. The first concerns information clarity and logic. The second concerns delivery and organization. Let's turn our attention to clarity and logic first. Individuals require their facts to be accurate, clearly represented, and logically coherent. Both the automatic and analytic systems benefit from these aspects. There are four communication points to consider when illuminating clarity and logic:

1. Make facts memorable.
2. Don't rely on facts alone.
3. Use assertions well.
4. Scrub or convert terminology.

I will presume you have uncovered the best data you can, have considered it well, and have completed your due diligence against your automatic system biases. When you have done your homework and are communicating with others, even those who daily shoulder your enterprise's responsibilities, you need to keep these four communication points in mind.

# Make Facts Memorable

While the facts may not be boring, you might be. Some leaders communicate important information in monotones or with poorly constructed visual data representations. When they use written communication, these problems are compounded. A lot of factual information is mundane, but it is often vital that it inform, persuade, or ignite. A low-energy communicator with a discordant array of data may thoroughly understand which facts actually matter and may have a terrific grasp of analysis implications, yet he may be unable to convey this well to others.

I am not implying that every meeting or every occasion of factual information delivery is a state-of-the-union occasion. It is just the opposite. What I am saying is that overreliance upon the idea that because the data speak for themselves, others see the same data you do and react in appropriate ways as you do is fertile ground for confirmation bias and the four fatal assumptions to toss your leadership on the shoals.

Constituents' need data *interpretation,* not data *recitation.* I have seen far too many managers who have not effectively compose their communication fall back upon the one set of information they can convey. By doing this they end up with recitations of data sets, sometimes running the length of a Wagnerian opera. This is a deadly communication situation. Have you ever been in a meeting when some leader is dazzling others with her command of not just the quantitative facts, but the contextual ideas, facts concerning trends and the mood of the workforce? This reliance on virtuoso performances of your knowledge gets in the way of helping others see the facts that are most meaningful. If the fundamental essence of your leadership communication is your ability to simply recite data, then prepare to have your role outsourced to a computer.

Visual comparisons, amazing facts, animated time series, simple but colorful charts, and other techniques can elevate and obscure information. I agree with Edward Tufte, respected master of the visual display of quantitative data, that graphics are not "devices for showing the obvious to the ignorant."[7]

There is an unfortunate tendency for too many of us to allow spreadsheet software default settings to illustrate important data. The default setting is the same as a base coat of paint in your home. Few of us would find leaving things at that stage satisfying. The visual display of quantitative data is a discipline we admire when we encounter brilliant examples, but few of us are willing to raise our game in its usage. Some simply use bullet lists or tables as their sole range of expertise to represent ideas. There are times when these approaches are necessary and even beneficial, especially if time is more important than impact, or if the information itself is merely an update when the important facts have already been highlighted. However, a lack of time and inattention often buries important information, doesn't provide data contrast, or inadvertently distorts information. As Nathan Yau states in his book *Visualize This*, "At some point in time, lies and statistics became almost synonymous, but it's not the numbers that lie. It's the people who use the numbers who lie. Sometimes it's on purpose to serve an agenda, but most of the time it's inadvertent. When you don't know how to create a graph properly or communicate with data in an unbiased way, false junk is likely to sprout."[8]

Techniques for making facts memorable include the use of amazing facts, comparative illustrations, animated time series, and well-constructed visual displays. Each of these can be rendered simply and in a short time. Each of them repay the effort in order to highlight the data worth considering. Deciding how much time to put into using these tools is tricky in a fast-paced world. Those leaders who more regularly devote time and attention to the boring aspects of the facts enhance their leverage ability and help overcome the three communication resistances.

Here's an illustration of an amazing fact. How many rivers in the world are longer than 1,000 miles, or 1,600 kilometers? As your mind rolls through its available information about this, I'll tell you where I'm going. Humans love novelty, they enjoy surprise, and these sparks of interest have attention-grabbing power. My experience with many groups of people over the past few years tells me you are more likely to guess in the neighborhood of five to twelve rivers than two hundred rivers. In my experience no one has guessed the right answer, but some have ventured wild guesses simply because they suspect the answer can't be just a few. And they are right. There are seventy-six rivers in the world longer than 1,000 miles.

It could be that I use this surprising tidbit to rivet your attention to my topic of long, navigable waterways in the world. The number sparks your interest, which allows me to elaborate. I could also use this data point as a stepping-stone to the real information I want you to see, which is that twenty of these rivers, nearly a third, run through Russia. And this second level of novelty allows me to bring your attention into even finer focus.

Vivid comparisons can also help. I recently started exercising more regularly than I had in years (the recession granted me some extra free time). It helped me lose some unwanted weight, especially around the middle. Last Thanksgiving some extended family members visited and were commenting on my slimmer profile. I was pleased they noticed and said I had lost twenty pounds. One of them immediately said, "Wow, you carved a turkey off your gut!"

Another comparison that helps make data memorable can be used to make hard-to-understand references more understandable. The Richter earthquake scale is one of those exponential scales that confuse most of us. We know that a seven on the scale is bad and that a nine on the scale is much worse, but because the actual numbers seven and nine have a linear relationship nearly all the time, we don't know how to comprehend the impact. A method for visualizing the comparison might take this form.

Remember the terrible Haitian earthquake in January 2010? It registered a 7.0. The March 2011 earthquake that rocked Japan with a tsunami registered nearly a 9.0. In order to understand the exponential effects, we need to move from a linear view to a three-dimensional view to show the relative strength of the earthquakes. Three dimensions, or volume, make exponential scales easier to understand. If the Haitian earthquake were the size of a golf ball, the Japanese earthquake would be a beach ball. Golf balls and beach balls are familiar enough three-dimensional objects to help make this comparison work and help others visualize the impact more clearly. You could even extend the reference scale. A 7.0 is a golf ball, an 8.0 is a soccer ball, and a 9.0 is a beach ball. Using a visual image extends the recall effects of the illustration.

Time series data can be referenced as a series of static graphs that show change over specific time periods. However, turning the few single snapshots of change over time into a smoothly flowing movie illustrates the data in much more memorable manner. The automatic system is tickled pink and the analytic system isn't offended. I once saw a thirty-second movie that showed the increase in unemployment in the United States from 2007 to 2010 that told an entire story in less time than it would take to print the charts. A county map of the United States showed by color the level of unemployment at the beginning of 2007. Lighter colors indicated low unemployment and darker colors indicated higher unemployment. In 2007 the chart was light with a few medium-dark spots. Over the thirty seconds, I watched nearly the entire country go dark. Time series overviews like this engage our automatic *and* analytic logical processes. Because the automatic system is satisfied by the coherence of the imagery, the analytic system can engage in peering more closely into specific data sets it wants to probe.

## Don't Rely on Facts Alone

Facts alone seldom persuade and rarely inspire. Chip Heath and Dan Heath in their book, *Made to Stick: Why Some Ideas Survive and Others Die* (which is organized around the ideas of facts, credibility, emotionality, and stories—another confirmation of my 1990s research), use a wide variety of examples about how to make your data come alive. Their ideas about concreteness, surprise, emotional relevance, and the use of stories as methods to make information, ideas, policies, and modes of thought stick in people's minds are well considered and wonderfully interesting.[9]

Kenneth Hammond, former director of the Center for Judgment and Policy at the University of Colorado at Boulder, spent his academic career demonstrating how our minds race from more automatic or intuitive judgments to more analytic processes for rendering judgments. He makes a clear distinction between two meta-theories of thought on the factual channel. One is the correspondence theory, which is largely concerned with accuracy. The facts of a judgment must be accurate and correspond to the judgment. Coherence theories "demand that the facts 'hang together,' that they tell a good story, one that is plausible and compelling because there are no discordant elements."[10] When we use facts only to satisfy accuracy, we default to letting the facts speak for themselves. To speak for the facts we need to add emotion, energy, and excitement.

In *The Art of the Long View*, Peter Schwartz recounts a telling story about this dynamism between accuracy and coherence. He relates the early days of scenario analysis at Royal Dutch/Shell, a company that was considered the weakest of the top seven oil companies during the 1960s. After the Six-Day War in the Middle East in 1967, the relatively new and somewhat tentative OPEC nations began to consider flexing their economic muscles. Pierre Wack and Ted Newland at Royal Dutch/Shell, as part of their strategic planning unit, began to see that OPEC could command higher prices for their oil. The only question was when they would initiate the new prices. Wack and Newland assembled their executives and presented the information they had gathered in the traditional manner: contrasting current trends with contingency trends. They delivered their findings in a basic, data-driven style devoid of any energy, emotion, or excitement. They were victims of hoping the data would speak for themselves.

The executives took in the information and did not change one course of action. Wack was shocked that they so cavalierly disregarded his rigorous data-mining and analysis. He decided he had to make the managers feel the shock of what the future would likely become. "[He] warned the drillers and explorers who sought new oil to get ready for the possibility that OPEC countries would take over the oil fields. Most importantly, Pierre vividly pointed to the forces in the world, and what sorts of influences those forces had to have. He helped managers imagine the decisions they might have to make as a result."[11] This time the executives heard the facts (some of whom wondered why Wack hadn't spoken up earlier). As a result, Shell rapidly became one of the top two oil companies in the years immediately following, because Wack's message had gotten through.

The second presentation got through to the executives, and they were emotionally and strategically prepared for the 1973 collective actions of OPEC that led to the so-called energy crisis. This sense of the facts not speaking for themselves and the requirement to add sufficient energy and emotion to the facts has been around for some time. However, I still hear managers, even senior managers, complain to me about what their superiors demand from them in meetings and presentations. "Don't give me all that bullshit. Just tell me the facts. I'll decide." If executives at Royal Dutch/Shell had acted that way, the oil company rankings would look a bit different.

# Use Assertions Well

Not all facts on the factual channel are data points from a table, graph, or chart. Some are simple assertions, which our automatic and analytic minds accept as factual information. The assertions are processed as part of the logic of an argument and treated as any other factual information.

Goals are a common form of this assertion set. We set our sights upon a direction, probably quantify certain measures of that destination, and assert that's where we are going. When we assert that our business is to delight customers, to create the world's best workplace, or to "bring good things to life," these are processed more than just marketing slogans. They are assertions that appeal to ideals perhaps, but they are treated as logical variables. I've heard more than one argument among my clients as to whether or not they are living up to those assertions.

You need to use assertions well, with deliberation, candor, and caution. Because they are part of the factual channel, constituents will hold you accountable (notice the "counting" part of the word *accountable*) for progress toward those facts. When the *Challenger* space shuttle exploded in 1987, Reagan asserted that the space program would continue, that shuttle flights in particular would continue, and that there would be more civilians in space. His assertions were part of his overall belief that progress should not be stopped because of misfortune, even though this particular misfortune was grave and deserved the greatest of admiration and respect from a nation.

Before Reagan, John F. Kennedy asserted we should go to the moon. At his famous speech at Rich University when he was appealing to the nation for a manned space mission to the moon, he asserted that nations take up these challenges because they are hard, not easy. Havel, as I have mentioned before, asserted that the Czech Republic would take its place among European nations as a natural consequence of the government's dedication to its citizens. Mandela asserted in his inaugural that he would heal the wounds of the past while constructing a new order of justice. Assertions are statements that carry the weight of fact. Use them well.

# Scrub or Convert Terminology

We live in an age of increasing levels of complexity both in our terminology and in the number of new disciplines arising that craft new terminology. I have worked with a number of hospital systems over time, and it used to come as a surprise to me that medical terminology varied so much from discipline to discipline. However, I was not surprised at the disconnect between the terms used in providing health care and the terms used in the business of health care. While all systems develop a general enough type of terminology that works nearly everywhere in the system, this general terminology often does an inadequate job of identifying causal factors that affect decisions and motivations.

I just entered the word *jargon* into Amazon's search engine. The first dozen book suggestions it returned offered entire editions on how to understand the jargon of business, obscure dialects, philosophy, technology, the Internet, and the "salty" language of the Marine Corps. All disciplines have developed specialized language. There are good reasons they do. Jargon, inside a discipline, helps reduce complexity to easy-to-carry-around idea packets, promotes a sense of camaraderie, and shortens our communications to lengths that enable more action. It works the same way as Kahneman uses *System 1* and *System 2* and why I use *automatic* and *analytic*. The easy-to-remember terms stand for more complex ideas, but the easy terms are simpler to remember and retain. For example, we would not benefit from writing or saying *deoxyribonucleic acid* each time we discuss DNA. Nor would we likely use the term *DNA* as powerfully in a metaphoric sense if we did.

We all know the problem is communicating outside a more narrow discipline. Reducing, explaining, or converting specialized jargon into ideas, words, or metaphors that are easy for a general audience to understand is hard work. But if you want your data to be thoroughly understood, you need to do the work.

This leads me to supply an illustration of the HTT and HTH coin-toss scenario. Remember, the answer to which of the sequences occurs more regularly is HTT, not HTH, and they do not both occur with the same frequency. Providing a visual illustration will help you see why HTT happens more frequently. Start by looking at the figure that follows.

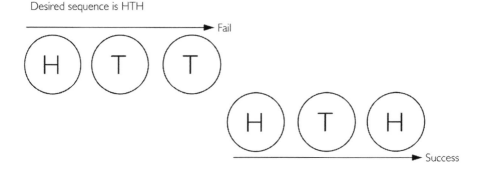

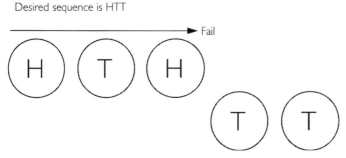

The first two rows of coin tossing show what happens if you are tossing for the HTH sequence. Let's say the first two tosses get you an H and T. The third toss could complete the sequence if its heads, but it comes up tails as shown. In order to get the HTH sequence, then, you have to start from the beginning.

The second two rows show what happens with the HTT sequence. If your first two tosses are an H and T, you hope for a third toss to yield a tails. If it yields a heads, you then only have to toss two tails in sequence to get a HTT sequence. This difference lets the HTT sequence on average appear after eight tosses while the average number of tosses to get HTH is ten.

# Use Easy-to-Remember Logical Structures

Turning our attention away from logic and clarity to delivery and organization brings us to the second aspect of the factual channel. You may have done your fact checking; worked on your jargon; and developed some great charts, graphs, or other illustrations for your facts, but have not organized them in a manner that allows others to easily follow your logical structure. If you want message throughput, you need to deliver your facts in such a manner that others can anticipate the conclusion before you arrive. You need to organize your facts into a familiar logical pattern. Great logic can be disguised, distorted, or diminished without considering how to arrange the facts so that others can follow the logic. There are a variety of methods for organizing the flow of your logical discourse. You may want to consider the following as templates you can use.

## Past/Present/Future

This is a classic timeline form of organizing an argument. Many different time series displays can be used as aids to this organizing principle. Just be careful that past conclusions are reconsidered in the light of present circumstances. I have already discussed this particular strategy as a key component of your central movie. It also applies to snippets of that central movie as well.

## Pro/Con

Most of us have conducted this analysis when weighing important considerations. It can be an effective way to communicate a decision, especially when a dilemma has been presented. A historic example of this kind of reasoning can be found in a letter from Benjamin Franklin to Joseph Priestly (a pastor, a contemporary of Franklin's, an inventor, and among those credited with the discovery of oxygen):

London, Sept. 19, 1772

Dear Sir,
In the affair of so much importance to you, wherein you ask my advice, I cannot, for want of sufficient premises, advise you what to determine, but if you please I will tell you how. When those difficult cases occur, they are difficult, chiefly because while we have them under

consideration, all the reasons pro and con are not present to the mind at the same time; but sometimes one set present themselves, and at other times another, the first being out of sight. Hence the various purposes or inclinations that alternatively prevail, and the uncertainty that perplexes us. To get over this, my way is to divide half a sheet of paper by a line into two columns; writing over the one Pro, and over the other Con. Then, during three or four days consideration, I put down under the different heads short hints of the different motives, that at different times occur to me, for or against the measure. When I have thus got them all together in one view, I endeavor to estimate their respective weights; and where I find two, one on each side, that seem equal, I strike them both out. If I find a reason pro equal to some two reasons con, I strike out the three. If I judge some two reasons con, equal to three reasons pro, I strike out the five; and thus proceeding I find at length where the balance lies; and if, after a day or two of further consideration, nothing new that is of importance occurs on either side, I come to a determination accordingly. And, though the weight of the reasons cannot be taken with the precision of algebraic quantities, yet when each is thus considered, separately and comparatively, and the whole lies before me, I think I can judge better, and am less liable to make a rash step, and in fact I have found great advantage from this kind of equation, and what might be called moral or prudential algebra. Wishing sincerely that you may determine for the best, I am ever, my dear friend, yours most affectionately.
B. Franklin[12]

# Cause/Effect

This is the brass ring of reasoning. Many business decisions are based upon trend analysis, correlated data, and circumstantial evidence, because finding true cause-and-effect relationship is empirically difficult to calculate. Use with caution. Or if you intend to use cause/effect relationships in a loose manner, let your audience know that you are reasoning from cause/effect based upon some assumptions that may or may not be as provable as you would like. Just because a cause/effect rationale cannot be nailed down to the fifth decimal doesn't mean this form of connecting-the-dots reasoning is necessarily bad.

## Break-Even

This is a much-used method of helping constituents see where an important tipping point or change might occur. It also helps them recognize the accompanying shift in behavior that is required to capitalize on the opportunity.

## Lesser of Two Evils

This is particularly a good organizing principle when a difficult decision has been reached regarding loss. It is often used during situations such as downsizing, reallocating resources, restructuring facilities, or mergers.

## Right vs. Wrong and Right vs. Right

These two forms of reasoning are used primarily when moral or ethical issues are at stake. Determining if a decision is morally correct or not (right vs. wrong) can be easy and enormously difficult. Displaying the various steps of consideration in a right vs. wrong decision manner can help guide others through the reasoning process used to derive an answer. Right vs. right decision making is often even harder, because a leader is attempting to choose between two positively held values. Perhaps the most common example of this is choosing between the financial and social responsibilities an organization bears.

## Dissuasion

This is the classic method of arguing from an opposite point of view. It is a way of pointing at what you want by communicating what you do not want. Leo Burnett, the famed marketing and advertising genius of the highly regarded Leo Burnett Company, used this organizing principle for his valedictory address when he retired. Delivered on December 1, 1967, it was titled "When to Take My Name Off the Door." The entire speech is worth a read, but below are excerpts that showcase this form of reasoning from the opposite.

But let me tell you when I might demand that you take my name off the door. That will be the day when you spend more time trying to make money and less time making advertising—our kind of advertising. When you forget that the sheer fun of ad making and the lift you get out of it—the creative climate of the place—should be as important as money to the very special breed of writers and artists and business professionals who compose this company of ours—and make it tick. When you lose that restless feeling that nothing you do is ever quite good enough.

When you lose your itch to do the job well for its own sake -regardless of the client, or the money or the effort it takes.

When you lose your passion for thoroughness . . . your hatred of loose ends.

When you stop reaching for the manner, the overtone, the marriage of words and pictures that produces the fresh, the memorable and the believable effect . . .

Finally, when you lose your respect for the lonely man—the man at his typewriter or his drawing board or behind his camera or just scribbling notes with one of our big black pencils—or working all night on a media plan. When you forget that the lonely man—and thank God for him—has made the agency we now have possible. When you forget he's the man who, because he is reaching harder, sometimes actually gets hold of—for a moment—one of those hot, unreachable stars.[13]

# Classic W

This is the most commonly taught storytelling method taught in creative writing classes. The shape of the letter "W" describes how it works. Most stories begin at the upper left of the "W." The stage is set and the main characters and background are established. Then the story takes a dive downward (first downward stroke of the letter). A problem arises, a crisis forms, or a series of challenges are formulated (evil comes to town). The business or individual rebounds from these, and it appears that it or he will be victorious (middle of the "W"). But then another, perhaps even graver problem arises, and the company or individual is plunged back down (evil has more problems up its sleeve). However, in the end, the business or individual succeeds. An interesting number of case studies follow this general form.

## Journalistic

This one is simple and straightforward. This organizing idea answers the questions who, what, when, where, why, and how.

# Summary

People love facts. We gobble and regurgitate sports statistics, weather data, calorie counts, business indicators, and gas prices. Factoid junkies play trivia games. Investors breathlessly track the rise and fall of a selection of their favorite market indicators on a minute-by-minute basis, updating their favorite mental model of how the stock market works. We are media-bludgeoned by the latest facts on crime, trade imbalances, pollen counts, death tolls, hair loss, and box office records. Some people will never know who won last night's game while others know individual players' middle names, scoring average, lifetime league ranking, and high school mascot. Even though individuals track different facts or track facts differently, we are all tuned to the factual channel.

Our automatic system is always on, and it makes up stories about what's happening in the world that we believe, even when we know we should not. A familiar example of this is perhaps the lucky streak phenomenon. In any sport or gaming activity, our automatic systems are persuaded that individuals' abilities run in patterns of lucky and unlucky streaks. When we encounter one of these patterns we ask the sports player to keep going until the luck runs out, we keep doubling down at blackjack because we believe we will win, and we keep using the same sales pitch regardless of the customer we encounter because we are riding a lucky streak.

Our analytic streak knows that all of these streaks are simply statistical phenomena and that relying on our faulty automatic systems is perilous. By and large, though, it takes mental effort to convince our automatic systems to pay attention to the more reflective and probably better analysis. This is where your factual channel requires your greatest attention. As a leader, when you have distilled judgment from carefully reasoned facts and have answers that can update the automatic system's wanderings, you need to present your facts in such a manner that your constituents' automatic and analytic systems are both satisfied. To do this requires not just great numbers or raw data, as such information surely cannot speak for itself. It requires you to organize and deliver your hard-won analysis using interesting facts to rivet attention, energy to add to dimension, and logical stories to keep the data hanging together.

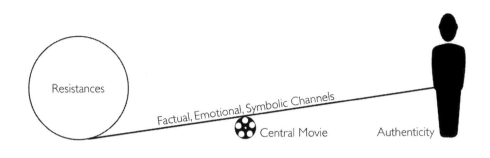

Resistances

Factual, Emotional, Symbolic Channels

Central Movie

Authenticity

# PRACTICE

Pablo Casals is considered the best cellist of the first half of the twentieth century and one of the greatest known in modern history. He started music studies very early in life and at the age of thirteen found sheet music for Bach's six cello suites in a Barcelona music shop. He started practicing them and made his first public performance of one of them at the age of twenty-six. He didn't want to play before he was ready. He played at London's Crystal Palace, at the summer home of Queen Victoria, and twice at the White House—once for Theodore Roosevelt and once for John F. Kennedy. Few in history can claim a reputation that spans such a length of time When Casals was ninety-one, a young music student found him rehearsing alone and asked him why in the world he continued to practice. The famed cellist replied, "Because I am making progress."[1]

Communication requires the same devotion if you want your leadership to rise above the ordinary. Even if you have a senior role in politics, are an officer of a renowned corporation, or are the head of a public sector charity, you need to continue making communication progress. I hope this slim volume has helped you see that much of what you have already learned, largely through experience, is useful and that by practicing certain very particular ideas your communication will provide greater leverage. Our knowledge of what makes a leader's voice work is far more extensive and accurate than it's ever been. Throughout history science has informed art, and the art of communication is no exception to this rule.

The rate of change is rapid. For example, many adults I speak with today still resurrect a movie from memory about neurology that's based upon a left-brain/right-brain schematic popularized in the 1980s. Science is not static, however, and that model is woefully outdated. As John Medina writes, "You have probably heard the term left brain vs. right brain. You may have heard that this underscores creative vs. analytical people. That's a folk tale, the equivalent of saying the left side of a luxury liner is responsible for keeping the ship afloat, and the right is responsible for making it move through the water. Both sides are involved in both processes."[2]

Training in platform skills communication, comprised of largely modern interpretations of anecdotal evidence, is surprisingly helpful when teaching those who have few or no communication skills. But communication understanding has progressed, just like neurology, leaving many of those traditional platform skills techniques up for scrutiny. Aristotle's methods of rhetoric were the gold standard until about 150 years ago, and many of his thoughts still echo in modern rhetorical studies. Modern versions of rhetoric have updated his thesis and improved upon it, but rhetoric often feels like memorizing the properties of every one of the periodic table elements without first studying the very few fundamental particles that create all elements. I have tried to approach communication in this book by looking at the fundamentals.

Public relations firms and media specialists have formed a body of knowledge concerning two aspects of leadership communication. The former teach you how to communicate without saying anything that will get you into trouble, and the latter teach you how to manipulate others to buy your product or support your cause. Both specialties have their place, but those same skills work poorly on constituents who have willingly joined you in your cause, political campaign, or corporate endeavor. Your constituency, which includes your customers these days, denounces manipulation, and its members will create their own movies of what you are up to if your PR communiqués are insufficient, meaning not creating a full high-definition movie using the three channels. Litigation fears and other pressures of self-protection may at times warrant vagueness, but you should not imagine that this provides leverage in an age where anyone with access to the Internet can investigate. The emperor with no clothes can be exposed in the length of time it takes to conduct an Internet search.

I chose the principle of the lever to connect four fundamentals: (1) authenticity, (2) your key messages or central movie, (3) the leverage of three-channel communication, and (4) overcoming the most common resistances. These four pieces of communication dynamics tell a very large story. Your movie will not be respected if you suffer a breach of integrity or credibility; it will not be heard at all if you have no key ideas or central movie. If you use only one or two of the channels, others will create a different movie from the one you are conveying, and even if you provide an authentic, HD-quality three-channel central movie, you may still struggle to overcome the most persistent forms of congeniality bias.

## A Few Words about You

"The self that is the center of narrative gravity is constructed not only out of real-life materials; it is also organized around a set of aims, ideals, and aspirations of the self," writes Owen Flanagan.[3] His advanced degrees in psychology and neuroscience afford him a particularly acute view of these matters. This narrative gravity strikes at the heart of your communication to yourself, your self-talk, about who you really are. Self-understanding, in its most essential neurological form, concerns how we consciously and unconsciously communicate to ourselves.

V. S. Ramachandran, as I indicated in chapter 2, asserts five conditions that must be met for an individual to have a sense of self. These conditions correspond to my leverage model very directly. His first condition is an unbroken thread of experience; a knowledge and feeling of our past and present, and ideas of our future. These are part of the central movie, constructed by facts, emotions, and symbols. The second condition he mentions is a coherence, or unity of self. This idea attaches both to authenticity and the three channels. The word *integrity* relates to *integral* and *integer* from the same root word, meaning "one." Integrity is being one with yourself. Ramachandran's third and fourth conditions also deal with authenticity in that we must feel anchored to our physical bodies to have a sense of self. And we possess a sense of agency or free will, which means we can change our movies based upon experience, study, and persuasive arguments from others. And the fifth condition involves authenticity, the three-channels, and the central movie. We are creatures capable of self-reflection, capable of attending to our sense of narrative gravity, of reviewing and contemplating our own movies of ourselves. As Ramachandran puts it, "A self that's unaware of itself is an oxymoron."[4]

I mentioned Gardner's seven "Rs" in chapter 2. He asserts that the same seven ideas that help you influence a change in others' movies are the same seven required for you to change your own movie. His seven "Rs" easily line up with my leverage model, which means he and I agree on the processes that create the movies that affect your personal mind and how you communicate this movie to others to affect their minds.

If you are not convinced of your movie about yourself, your place to stand deteriorates from bedrock to quicksand. If you are not convinced of your movie, you will likely fall prey to one- or two-channel communication to convey it to others. You most frequently resort to one of these three methods:

1. Dazzling others with your data
2. Pounding others with an emotional appeal
3. Appealing to others' automatic system with a simple story

You can have some success with any one of these methods, but you will have squandered your potential leverageability by not using all three channels.

Without a sense of self you cannot generate purpose, strategy, or vision, nor can you find the motivational energy to sustain momentum. You are lost and others will not follow.

# The Leader's Voice

There are three great aspects of leadership: maintaining credibility, moving forward, and mobilizing others. These domains have been ratified repeatedly over the past century. Communication is the constant companion of most of the significant components of these three arenas.

Reading about communication is one way to update your movie and perhaps even change your mind. But reading isn't practicing. When I conduct two-day workshops, over 60 percent of the time investment is spent in practice, not absorbing information. Find any great leader, scientist, artist, adventurer, writer, athlete, musician, or any other category of occupation or devotion. and you will find a practitioner.

There are two keys to greatness: practice and practicing the right ideas or techniques. I hope I have provided you with encouragement for the first and information for the second.

# NOTES

## Chapter 1: Leadership Communication

1. Donald N. Sull and Charles Spinosa, "Promise-Based Management: The Essence of Execution," *Harvard Business Review* 85, no. 4 (2007): 81.
2. Warren Bennis, Burt Nana, and Burt Nanus, *Leaders: Strategies for Taking Charge* (New York: Harper Collins, 1985).
3. James MacGregor Burns, *Leadership* (New York: Harper and Row, 1978), 469.
4. Kathleen Hall Jamieson, *Eloquence in an Electronic Age: The Transformation of Political Speechmaking* (Oxford: Oxford University Press, 1988), 10–11.
5. Boris Groysber, Andrew N. McLean, and Nitin Nohria, "Are Leaders Portable?" *Harvard Business Review*, March 2006.
6. William W. George, *Authentic Leadership: Rediscovering the Secrets to Creating Lasting Value* (San Francisco: Jossey-Bass, 2003), 11.
7. Peter Georgescu, *The Source of Success* (San Francisco: Jossey-Bass, 2005), 116.
8. IABC, "Only One-Third of Companies Say Their Employees Understand and Live Business Strategy in Daily Jobs," International Association of

Business Communicators, September 13, 2005, http://news.iabc.com/index.php?s=press_releases&item=19, accessed November 6, 2007.

9. Towers Perrin Global Workforce Study 2007–2008, "Closing the Engagement Gap: A Road Map for Driving Superior Business Performance," http://www.towersperrin.com/tp/getwebcachedoc?webc=HRS/USA/2008/200803/GWS_Global_Report20072008_31208.pdf, accessed August 30, 2011.

10. IABC, "Only One-Third of Companies."

11. Archimedes quote, ThinkExist.com, http://thinkexist.com/quotation/give_me_a_place_to_stand-and_i_will_move_the/289451.html, accessed October 11. 2011.

12. Margaret Thatcher quote, Brainy Quote, http://www.brainyquote.com/quotes/authors/m/margaret_thatcher_3.html, accessed January 6, 2012.

13. Nelson Mandela quote, Brainy Quote, http://www.brainyquote.com/quotes/authors/n/nelson_mandela.html, accessed January 6, 2012

14. Ho Chi Minh quote, Brainy Quote, http://www.brainyquote.com/quotes/authors/h/ho_chi_minh.html, accessed January 6, 2012.

15. Ronald Reagan quote, Brainy Quote, http://www.brainyquote.com/quotes/authors/r/ronald_reagan_3.html, accessed January 6, 2012.

16. John F. Kennedy quotes, from his inaugural address, The American Presidency Project, http://www.presidency.ucsb.edu/ws/index.php?pid=8032#axzz1ihApo0Uy, accessed January 6, 2012.

17. Aung San Suu Kyi quote, GoodReads.com, http://www.goodreads.com/author/quotes/61546.Aung_San_Suu_Kyi, accessed January 6, 2012.

18. Personal interview, circa 1987, Washington, D.C.

19. John W. Gardner, *On Leadership* (New York: Free Press 1990), 28–29.

20. Howard Gardner, *Leading Minds* (New York: Basic Books, 1985), 34.

# Chapter 2: The Moviemaking Brain

1. Dean Buonomano, *Brain Bugs: How The Brain's Flaws Shape Our Lives* (New York: W. W. Norton, 2011), Kindle edition.

2. Joel M. Podolny, Rakesh Khurana, and Marya L. Besharov, "Revisiting the Meaning of Leadership," in *Handbook of Leadership Theory and Practice: An*

*HBS Centennial Colloquium on Advancing Leadership*, ed. Nitin Nohria and Rakesh Khurana, 65–106 (Boston: Harvard Business School Publishing, 2010), 97.

3. Antonio Damasio, *Descartes' Error: Emotion, Reason, and the Human Brain* (New York: Grosset/Putnam, 1994), 31.

4. Ibid., 33–51.

5. Oliver Sacks, *The Man Who Mistook His Wife for a Hat: And Other Clinical Tales* (New York: HarperPerennial, 1970), 177–86.

6. Ibid., 183–84.

7. Ibid., 184.

8. John H. Ratey, *A User's Guide to the Brain: Perception, Attention, and the Four Theaters of the Brain* (New York: Vintage, 2002), 5.

9. Joseph LeDoux, *The Emotional Brain: The Mysterious Underpinnings of Emotional Life* (New York: Touchstone, 1996), 33.

10. V. S. Ramachandran, *A Brief Tour of Human Consciousness: From Imposter Poodles to Purple Numbers* (New York: Pi Press, 2004), 96.

11. Antonio Damasio, *Looking for Spinoza: Joy, Sorrow, and the Feeling Brain* (Orlando, FL: Harcourt, 2003), 198.

12. Ratey, *User's Guide*, 5.

13. Damasio, *Looking for Spinoza*, 194.

14. Richard S. Lazarus and Bernice N. Lazarus, *Passion and Reason: Making Sense of Our Emotions* (New York: Oxford University Press, 1996), 199.

15. Daniel Siegel, *The Developing Mind: How Relationships and the Brain Interact to Shape Who We Are* (New York: Guilford Press, 2001), 158.

16. LeDoux, *Emotional Brain*, 19.

17. Ratey, *User's Guide*, 186.

18. Damasio, *Looking for Spinoza*, 195.

19. LeDoux, *Emotional Brain*, 106.

20. Ian Tattersall, "Drenched in Symbolism," *Scientific American* 281, no. 1 (2003): 55.

21. George Lakoff and Mark Johnson, *Metaphors We Live By* (Chicago: University of Chicago Press, 1980), 257.

22. H. Gardner, *Leading Minds*, 65.

23. Steven Pinker, *How the Mind Works* (New York: W. W. Norton, 1996), 359.

24. Antonio Damasio, *The Feeling of What Happens: Body and Emotion in the Making of Consciousness* (New York: Harcourt Brace, 1999), 189.

25. Matt Ridley, *Nature Via Nurture: Genes, Experience, and What Makes Us Human* (New York: HarperCollins, 2003), 220.

26. Christine Kenneally, *The First Word: The Search for the Origins of Language* (New York: Viking, 2007), Kindle edition.

27. John Medina, *Brain Rules: 12 Principles for Surviving and Thriving at Work, Home, and School* (Seattle: Pear Press, 2008), Kindle edition.

28. Pinker, *How the Mind Works*, 552.

29. Quoted in Jessica Snyder Sachs, "A Spielberg in Your Own Mind," *Popular Science,* July 1, 2003, 52.

30. Ratey, *User's Guide*, 186.

31. Ibid.

32. Medina, *Brain Rules*.

33. Robert McKee, "Storytelling That Moves People," *Harvard Business Review* 81, no. 6 (2003): 52.

34. Howard Gardner, *Changing Minds: The Art and Science of Changing Our Own and Other Peoples' Minds* (Boston: Harvard Business School Publishing, 2005), 15–16.

35. Georgianne Smith, "Emotional, Symbolic, and Factual Dimensions of Leadership Communication," unpublished dissertation, Pepperdine University, Malibu, California, August 1977, 89.

36. Ping Ping Fu, et al., "The Impact of Societal Cultural Values and Individual Social Beliefs on the Perceived Effectiveness of Managerial Influence Strategies," *Journal of International Business Studies* 35, no. 4 (2004): 289.

37. William Shakespeare, *MacBeth* 5.5.19–28 (London: Wordsworth Editions, 2005), 97–98.

# Chapter 3: Your Central Movie

1. Barnaby J. Feder, "Peter F. Drucker, a Pioneer in Social and Management Theory, Is Dead at 95," *New York Times*, November 12, 2005.

2. John W. Gardner, *Self-Renewal: The Individual and the Innovative Society* (New York: Harper and Row, 1964), 117–29.

3. Peter Koestenbaum, *Leadership: The Inner Side of Greatness* (San Francisco: John Wiley and Sons, 2002), 6.

4. Charles Taylor, *The Ethics of Authenticity* (Cambridge, MA: Harvard University Press, 1992), 10.

5. Rob Goffee and Gareth Jones, *Why Should Anyone Be Led by You?* (Cambridge, MA: Harvard Business School Publishing, 2006), 5.

6. Manfred F. R. Kets de Vries, *The Leadership Mystique: Leading Behavior in the Human Enterprise* (London: Prentice Hall, 2001), 303–305.

7. Manfred F. R. Kets de Vries, *Leaders, Fools, and Imposters: Essays on the Psychology of Leadership* (San Francisco: Jossey-Bass, 1993), 42.

8. Jonathan Daniels, *The Man of Independence* (Columbia: University of Missouri Press, 1998), 347–48.

9. Ibid., 348.

10. James M. Kouzes and Barry Z. Posner, *The Leadership Challenge*, 4th ed. (San Francisco: Jossey-Bass, 2007), iii–iv.

11. Bill George, podcast interview, Dean's Executive Leadership Series, Pepperdine University, http://bschool.pepperdine.edu/dels/podcasts/archive06-07.htm#wgp, accessed October 19, 2011.

12. Lao Tzu quote, Brainy Quote, http://www.brainyquote.com/quotes/authors/l/lao_tzu.html, accessed October 19, 2011.

13. Marcus Aurelius quote, Brainy Quote, http://www.brainyquote.com/quotes/authors/m/marcus_aurelius.html, accessed October 19, 2011.

14. Thales of Miletus quote, Brainy Quote, http://www.brainyquote.com/quotes/authors/t/thales.html, accessed October 19, 2001.

15. Markus Buckingham quote, "The Truth about You," YouTube, http://www.youtube.com/watch?v=0TZnqiSpmYk, accessed October 19, 2011.

16. Abraham Maslow, *Towards a Psychology of Being,* 3rd ed. (New York: John Wiley and Sons, 1999), 6.

17. Timothy D. Wilson, *Strangers to Ourselves: Discovering the Adaptive Unconscious* (Boston: Harvard University Press, 2004), 16.

18. Marshall Goldsmith, *What Got You Here Won't Get You There: How Successful People Become Even More Successful* (New York: Hyperion, 2007), 113–20.

19. John F. Kennedy quote, Brainy Quote, http://www.brainyquote.com/quotes/keywords/truth_3.html, accessed January 12, 2012.

20. Arie de Geus, *The Living Company: Habits for Survival in a Turbulent Business Environment* (Boston: Harvard Business School Publishing, 1997), 11.

21. John Micklethwait and Adrian Wooldridge, *The Company: A Short History of a Revolutionary Idea* (New York: Modern Library, 2005), xv.

22. "Running Faster, Falling Behind: John Hagel III on How American Business Can Catch Up," Knowledge@Wharton, June 23, 2010, http://knowledge.wharton.upenn.edu/article.cfm?articleid=2523, accessed January 16, 2012.

23. Dr. Thomas N. Duening, "Continuous Value Creation in the Age of Innovation," http://cpd.asee.org/PDF/ciec08sessions/3_CPD224_Duening.pdf, accessed January 16, 2012.

24. McKinsey and Company (Tim Koller, Marc Goedhart, David Wessels), *Valuation: Measuring and Managing the Value of Companies,* 5th ed. (Hoboken, NJ: John Wiley and Sons, 2010), Kindle edition.

25. Peter Senge, Bryan Smith, Nina Kruschwitz, Joe Laur, and Sara Schley, *The Necessary Revolution: How Individuals and Organizations Are Working Together to Create a Sustainable World* (New York: Broadway Books, 2010), 11.

26. D. H. Ingvar, "Memory of the Future," *Human Neurobiology* 4, no. 3 (1985): 127–36.

27. Daniel L. Schacter, Donna Rose Addis, and Randy L. Buckner, "Remembering the Past to Imagine the Future: The Prospective Brain," *Neuroscience* 8 (September 2007): 660.

28. William Hart and Dolores Albarracín, "What I Was Doing Versus What I Did," *Psychological Science* 20, no. 2 (2009): 243.

29. Michael Gazzaniga, *The Mind's Past* (Berkeley: University of California Press, 2000), 141.

30. Václav Havel, "The Power of the Powerless," 1978, http://www.vaclavhavel.cz/showtrans.php?cat=clanky&val=72_aj_clanky.html&typ=HTML, accessed January 17, 2012.

31. Ibid. In *The Struggle for Europe,* William Hitchcock concluded, "Havel's powerful essay 'The Power of the Powerless' argued that simply by 'living in truth'—by pointing out the falsehood and the lies that perpetuated the

political system in Czechoslovakia—one could restore some humanity to oneself and one's neighbors" (302).

32. "Václav Havel, Playwright and President," *Economist* online, December 18, 2011, http://www.economist.com/blogs/easternapproaches/2011/12/vaclav-havel-memoriam, accessed January 17, 2012.

33. Václav Havel, "New Year's Address to the Nation," Prague, January 1, 1991.

34. Ibid.

35. H. Gardner, *Changing Minds*, 5.

# Chapter 4: Symbolic Channel

1. Paul H. Thibodeau and Lera Boroditsky, "Metaphors We Think With: The Role of Metaphor in Reasoning," *PLos ONE* 6, no. 2 (2011).

2. George Lakoff, "The Neurocognitive Self: Conceptual System Research in the Twenty-first Century and the Rethinking of What a Person Is," in *The Science of the Mind: 2001 and Beyond*, ed. Robert Solso and Dominic Massaro (Oxford: Oxford University Press, 1995), 229.

3. Alexis Madrigal, "Why Are Spy Researchers Building a 'Metaphor Program'?" *Atlantic*, online edition, May 25, 2011, http://www.theatlantic.com/technology/archive/2011/05/why-are-spy-researchers-building-a-metaphor-program/239402, accessed December 7, 2011.

4. Steven J. Mithen, *The Prehistory of the Mind: The Cognitive Origins of Art, Religion, and Science* (London: Thames and Hudson, 1996), 26.

5. George Lakoff and Mark Johnson, *Metaphors We Live By* (Chicago: University of Chicago Press), 55; emphasis in original.

6. Derek C. Penn, Keith J. Holyoak, and Daniel J. Povinelli, "Darwin's Mistake: Explaining the Discontinuity Between Human and Nonhuman Minds," *Behavioral and Brain Sciences* 31 (2008): 113.

7. Pinker, *How the Mind Works*, 359.

8. Susan Oyama, *Evolution's Eye: A Systems View of the Biology-Culture Divide* (Durham, NC: Duke University Press, 2000), 10.

9. Dennis Meredith, *Explaining Research: How to Reach Key Audiences to Advance Your Work* (Oxford: Oxford University Press, 2010).

10. Stephen Fidler, Matthew Dalton, and Brian Blackstone, "Tensions Rise at EU Summit," *Wall Street Journal* online, December 9, 2011, http://online. wsj.com/article/SB10001424052970203501304577086030233783036. html?mod=WSJ_hp_LEFTTopStories, accessed December 18, 2011.

11. Bee-Shyuan Chang, "Beauty as Their Business," *New York Times* online, December 7, 2011, http://www.nytimes.com/2011/12/08/fashion/making-beauty-their-business.html?_r=1&ref=fashion, accessed December 18, 2011.

12. *South China Morning Post* online, http://www.scmp.com/portal/site/ SCMP/menuitem.2c913216495213d5df646910cba0a0a0/?vgnextoid=3 967fdb4efb14310VgnVCM100000360a0a0aRCRD&vgnextfmt=teaser& ss=Companies+%26+Finance&s=Business, accessed December 18, 2011.

13. Any Bourrier, "China's Dark Power," *Le Monde Diplomatique,* English Edition, December 12, 2011, http://mondediplo.com/2011/12/12china, accessed December 18, 2011.

14. Matt Kaplan, "An Eye-Opening Fossil," *Nature* online, December 7, 2011, http://www.nature.com/news/an-eye-opening-fossil-1.9586, accessed December 18, 2011.

15. "Towards a Smarter Grid," *Science Friday*, hosted by Ira Flatow, podcast excerpt from original broadcast, January 14, 2011. Available at *Science Friday* archives, http://www.sciencefriday.com/program/archives/201101143.

16. Picasso quote, Brainy Quotes, http://www.brainyquote.com/quotes/ authors/p/pablo_picasso.html, accessed January 19, 2012.

17. Tom Peters, "The Brand Called You," *Fast Company*, August 31, 1997, digital copy, http://www.fastcompany.com/magazine/10/brandyou.html, accessed January 19, 2012.

18. "Top 100 American Speeches of the Twentieth Century," Infoplease, http:// www.infoplease.com/ipa/A0932561.html, accessed January 24, 2012.

19. Medina, *Brain Rules.*

20. Meredith, *Explaining Research*, 9.

21. Matt Ridley, *Genome: The Autobiography of a Species in 23 Chapters* (New York: HarperCollins, 1999); Nassem Taleb, *The Black Swan: The Impact of the Highly Improbable* (New York: Random House, 2007); Peter Georgescu, *The Source of Success* (San Francisco: Jossey-Bass, 2005); Patrick Lencioni, *The Five Temptations of a CEO* (San Francisco: Jossey-Bass, 1998), *The Five*

*Dysfunctions of a Team* (San Francisco: Jossey-Bass, 2005), and *The Four Obsessions of an Extraordinary Executive* (San Francisco: Jossey-Bass, 2000); Warren Bennis, *Organizing Genius: The Secrets of Creative Collaboration* (Reading, MA: Addison-Wesley, 1997); Tom Peters, *In Search of Excellence: Lessons from America's Best-Run Companies* (New York: Harper and Row, 1982).

22. Tom Kelley, *The Art of Innovation* (New York: Doubleday, 2001), 5.

23. Bronwyn Fryer, "Storytelling That Moves People: A Conversation with Screenwriting Coach Robert McKee," *Harvard Business Review* (June 2003): 55.

24. Jennifer Edson Escalas, "Self-Referencing and Persuasion: Narrative Transportation Versus Analytical Elaboration," *Journal of Consumer Research* 33, no. 4 (2007): 421–29.

25. Barry Lopez, *Crossing Open Ground* (New York: Vintage Books, 1989), 69.

26. J. Madison Davis, *Novelist's Essential Guide to Creating Plot* (Cincinnati: F & W Publications, 2000), 168; Blake Snyder, *Save the Cat! The Last Book on Screenwriting You'll Ever Need* (Google eBook) (Studio City, CA: Michael Weiss Productions, 2005), 25–26.

27. Doris Kearns Goodwin, *Team of Rivals: The Political Genius of Abraham Lincoln* (New York: Simon and Schuster, 2005), 150.

# Chapter 5: Emotional Channel

1. Joseph LeDoux, *The Emotional Brain: The Mysterious Underpinnings of Emotional Life* (New York: Touchstone, 1996), 19.

2. Quoted in Siegel, *Developing Mind*, 123.

3. LeDoux, *Emotional Brain*, 114.

4. Robert Plutchik's Wheel of Emotions, http://en.wikipedia.org/wiki/File:Plutchik-wheel.svg, accessed February 8, 2012. You can find more about Plutchik's work in his book *Emotions and Life: Perspectives from Psychology, Biology, and Evolution* (Washington, DC: American Psychiatric Association, 2003).

5. "Basic Emotions," Changing Minds, http://changingminds.org/explanations/emotions/basic%20emotions.htm, accessed February 9, 2012.

6. W. Gerrod Parrott, "Ur-Emotions and Your Emotions: Reconceptualizing Basic Emotions," *Emotion Review* 2, no. 1 (2012): 14–21.

7. Antonio Damasio, *Looking for Spinoza: Joy, Sorrow, and the Feeling Brain* (Orlando, FL: Harcourt, 2003), 28.

8. Daniel Goleman, *Social Intelligence: The New Science of Human Relationships* (New York: Bantam, 2006), 5.

9. Damasio, *Looking for Spinoza*, 48.

10. Daniel Goleman, Richard Boyatzis, and Annie McKee, "Primal Leadership: The Hidden Driver of Great Performance," *Harvard Business Review,* December 2001, 51.

11. James H. Fowler and Nicholas Christakis, *British Medical Journal,* "Dynamic Spread of Happiness in a Large Social Network: Longitudinal Analysis over Twenty Years in the Framingham Heart Study," December 4, 2008, 337.

12. Alison L. Hill, David G. Rand, Martin A. Nowak, Nicholas A. Christakis, "Infectious Disease Modeling of Social Contagion in Networks," *PLoS Computational Biology,* November 2010.

13. Interview with iRobot Corporation co-founder and chairman Helen Greiner, *Science Friday,* NPR, February 4, 2005.

14. John D. Mayer, as quoted in "Leading by Feel," *Harvard Business Review,* January 2004, 28.

15. Jamieson, *Eloquence in an Electronic Age,* 182.

16. Matthew D. Lieberman, Naomi I Eisenberger, Molly J. Crockett, Sabrina M. Tom, Jennifer H. Pfeifer, and Baldwin M. Way, "Putting Feelings Into Words: Affect Labeling Disrupts Amygdala Activity in Response to Affective Stimuli," *Psychological Science* 18, no. 5 (2007): 421–28.

17. Valerie Manusov and Miles L. Patterson, *The Sage Handbook of Nonverbal Communication* (Thousand Oaks, CA: Sage Publications, 2006), 86.

18. Arthur M. Glenberg, "Introduction to the Mirror Neuron Forum," *Perspectives on Psychological Science* 6, no. 4 (2011), http://pps.sagepub.com/content/6/4/363.extract, accessed February 9, 2012.

19. V. S. Ramachandran, "The Neurons That Shaped Civilization," November 2009, TED.com, http://www.ted.com/talks/lang/en/vs_ramachandran_the_neurons_that_shaped_civilization.html, accessed February 9, 2012.

20. Jeremy I. Skipper, Howard C. Nusbaum, and Steven L. Small, "Listening to Talking Faces: Motor Cortical Activation during Speech Perception," *Neuroimage* 25, no. 1 (2005): 76–89.
21. Robert Spunt and Matthew Lieberman, "An Integrative Model of the Neural Systems Supporting the Comprehension of Observed Emotional Behavior," *NeuroImage* (2011): 6, available at http://www.scn.ucla.edu/pdf/Spunt(InPress)NeuroImage.pdf.
22. Michael Tomasello, *Origins of Human Communications* (Cambridge: MIT Press, 2008), Kindle edition.
23. Natalie Angier, "Deaf Babies Use Their Hands to Babble, Researcher Finds," *New York Times* online, March 22, 1991, http://www.nytimes.com/1991/03/22/us/deaf-babies-use-their-hands-to-babble-researcher-finds.html, February 11, 2012.
24. Margalit Fox, *Talking Hands: What Sign Language Reveals about the Mind* (New York: Simon and Schuster, 2007).
25. Paul Ekman, "Emotional and Conversational Nonverbal Signals," PaulEkman.com, http://www.paulekman.com/wp-content/uploads/2009/02/Emotional-And-Conversational-Nonverbal-Signals.pdf, accessed February 10, 2012.
26. Siegel, *Developing Mind,* 328.
27. Maneul Martín-Loeches, Alejandra Sel, Pilar Casado, Laura Jiménez, and Luis Castellanos, "Encouraging Expressions Affect the Brain and Alter Visual Attention," *PLos One* 4, no. 6 (2009): 1.
28. Ibid., 6.
29. Joseph LeDoux, *The Synaptic Self: How Our Brains Become Who We Are* (New York: Penguin, 2002), 174.

# Chapter 6: Factual Channel

1. Buonomano, "Brain Bugs."
2. Daniel Kahneman, *Thinking, Fast and Slow* (Paris: Farrar, Straus and Giroux, 2011), Kindle edition.

3. Brooks Jackson and Kathleen Hall-Jamieson, *UnSpun: Finding Facts in a World of Disinformation* (New York: Random House, 2007), x, xi.

4. Kahneman, *Thinking, Fast and Slow*.

5. "Peter Donnelly Shows How Stats Fool Juries," TED, July 2005, http://www.ted.com/talks/peter_donnelly_shows_how_stats_fool_juries.html, accessed February 27, 2012.

6. Jackson W. Granholm, "How to Design a Kludge," *Datamation* (February 1962): 30–31; available at http://neil.franklin.ch/Jokes_and_Fun/Kludge.html.

7. Scott Rosenberg, "The Data Artist," Salon.com, http://www1.salon.com/march97/tufte970310.html, accessed March 12, 2012.

8. Nathan Yau, *Visualize This: The FlowingData Guide to Design, Visualization, and Statistics* (New York: Wiley, 2011), xxi.

9. Chip Heath and Dan Heath, *Made to Stick: Why Some Ideas Survive and Others Die* (New York: Random House, 2007).

10. Kenneth Hammond, *Human Judgment and Social Policy: Irreducible Uncertainty, Inevitable Error, and Unavoidable Injustice* (New York: Oxford University Press, 1996), Kindle edition.

11. Peter Schwartz, *The Art of the Long View: Paths to Strategic Insight for Yourself and Your Company* (New York: Doubleday, 1991), Kindle edition.

12. "Benjamin Franklin's 1772 Letter to Joseph Priestley," ProCon.org, http://www.procon.org/franklinletter.htm, accessed December 5, 2007.

13. "Great Moments in Advertising: Leo Burnett's Speech," Branding Strategy Insider, October 28, 2007, http://www.brandingstrategyinsider.com/2007/10/great-moments-3.html, accessed March 12, 2012.

# Chapter 7: Practice

1. Norman Doidge, *The Brain That Changes Itself: Stories of Personal Triumph from the Frontiers of Science* (New York: Penguin, 2007), Kindle edition.

2. Medina, *Brain Rules*.

3. Owen Flanagan, *The Problem of the Soul* (New York: Basic Books, 2002), 251.

4. Ramachandran, *Brief Tour*, 96.

# ABOUT THE AUTHOR

Ronald Crossland has been in the leadership development field for over twenty years and is co-author of *The Leader's Voice: How Your Communication Can Inspire Action and Get Results!* (New York: Selectbooks, 2002, 2nd ed. 2008) and *The Leadership Experience: From Individual Success to Organizational Significance* (New York: Selectbooks, 2007). He holds a BS in Electronics Engineering Technology and an MBA from Oklahoma State University. Please continue to find information about how to improve your voice at his website, www.roncrossland.com.

Made in the USA
San Bernardino, CA
06 June 2017